Golf
Insidethe**Game**

Derek Lawrenson

Published in 1998 by Icon Books Ltd,
Grange Road, Duxford, Cambridge CB2 4QF
e-mail: icon@mistral.co.uk

Distributed in the UK, Europe, Canada, South Africa and Asia
by the Penguin Group:
Penguin Books Ltd, 27 Wrights Lane, London W8 5TZ

Published in Australia in 1998 by Allen & Unwin Pty Ltd,
PO Box 8500, 9 Atchison Street, St. Leonards, NSW 2065

ISBN 1 84046 030 X

Series edited by Sport and Leisure Books Ltd
Layout and illustrations: Zoran Jevtic, Audiografix
Cover design by Zoran Jevtic and Jeremy Cox
Photographs supplied by Colorsport

Printed and bound in Great Britain by
Biddles Ltd, Guildford and King's Lynn

CONTENTS

INTRODUCTION   4

HISTORY   6

RULES AND ETIQUETTE   27

GLOSSARY   51

HOW IT IS PLAYED   91

THE MODERN GAME   124

Facts and Figures   157

Miscellaneous   165

About the Author   172

Index   174

In my office at home I have six shelves groaning under the weight of at least 400 golf books and therefore, at the beginning of this one, it is only fair to address certain questions. Like: why add to the number? What can possibly be written about golf that has not appeared elsewhere? Haven't we seen a few insider's guides to golf in the past, if not exactly marketed under that title?

Certainly the answer to the last question has to be yes. It is also true that several subjects in golf have been recycled many more times than is good for them.

But equally, think for a moment about what has happened in the sport over the last five years and what is going to happen over the next five. When people talked in 1990 about being on line they were talking about a drive down the middle of the fairway, not visiting a web site. When Jose-Maria Olazabal won the Masters in 1994 he was the first player to win a major championship using a metal wood; now no one leaves home without one. Whoever wins the Players' Championship in 2002 will receive a first prize that will be roughly equivalent to what the total prize money was just ten years ago.

In other words, we are living through a period of change so dramatic that golf has experienced nothing like it. In America the sport is fast catching up the traditional pastimes of baseball, football and basketball in terms of popularity on television. As ever in Britain we are lagging some way behind but we'll get there.

And so: ever watched the Ryder Cup but wondered what on earth the commentators are on about, bandying about arcane terms that make golf sound like a foreign language? What about the sport's hidden meanings, the subtleties that make matchplay a totally different game from strokeplay? The tournaments that really matter when every event in the Sky canon is called prestigious?

Ever wondered what Nick Faldo is trying to do with a deliberate fade but never fancied wading through acres of instruction tomes to find out? This book is for you.

Ever asked yourself why a five iron instead of a six iron, why persimmon wood drivers have suddenly disappeared off the face of the earth, why golf has suddenly become hip and trendy? Ever watched the Masters or the Ryder Cup and thought: yes, I would like to know a bit more about this sport, how it ticks, how it functions, I'd like someone to put their arm around my shoulder and guide me with wit and a touch irreverently around its traditions and machinations? This book is definitely for you.

Most golf books are written with a reverence normally reserved for describing a religion. It does not have to be this way; indeed it is possible to write about the sport while taking into account that we are on the cusp of the twenty-first century rather than the twentieth. It is just that, when it comes to books, few people in Britain appear to have tried.

It is, admittedly, a fine balancing act. The last thing that anyone who is passionate about golf would seek to do would be to debunk its traditions. However, I believe that we can take a 1990s perspective on the sport and its traditions, and that is what I will attempt to do in this book.

More than ever, sport has become important in people's lives. As I write this, the Queen dominates the front page of the *Daily Telegraph* talking about the virtues of sport. Imagine that happening a decade ago? Me neither.

Much has been written in recent times about the modernising of the Royal Family. In its own small way, this book seeks to play its part in golf's modernisation. And I promise you: that is something you will not find in any other golf book.

Golf is often considered the most traditional of sports and in some ways it is. The Open Championship, for example, has always been played on a course built on land reclaimed from the sea – a links course, to use the common vernacular; the winner of the Masters each April at Augusta continues to be awarded a green jacket that might have looked fashionable when first presented in the 1930s but which is now so garish that one is sometimes left wondering if it would not be preferable to finish runner-up.

In other ways, though, the game has changed at such a clatter that tradition has been left battered and bruised in the stampede. In particular, the way the game has embraced the benefits of new technology has been quite staggering. Offer a man in his fifties a new computer and and he will part with his old one only after a mightily petulant bout of kicking and screaming. Yet offer the same man a shiny metal wood and the effect could not be more dramatic if the object in front of him was a dazzling mini-skirted blond. His own metal wood will be dumped in some forgotten corner, never – fingers crossed – to be used again.

I sometimes feel like I am the last golfer in the world who is still using woods that are made from – glory be – wood. But one only has to rewind the clock a dozen years to return to an age when no one had even heard of the manufacturer Callaway, let alone have one of their metal products stuffed in the golf bag; more remarkable still, it was not until Jose-Maria Olazabal in 1994 at Augusta that a professional won a major championship using a metal wood from the tee.

Now there is not a single participant who would

The right to the designation Royal – as conferred on a number of courses in the British Isles – is bestowed by the reigning King or Queen, or a member of the Royal house. The Perth Golfing Society was the first to receive it in 1833; the most recent was Royal Troon in 1978.

dream of entering a major without one, which is a rapid transformation by anyone's standards, let alone in a pastime considered traditional.

The last two players to change were Justin Leonard and Davis Love, and thereby hangs a tale about the inexorability of change. Leonard converted from metal to wood just before the 1997 Open Championship at Royal Troon and, as you might recall, the change worked rather well for him as he went on to win.

Love, meanwhile, was so impressed by Leonard's successful conversion that he decided to change before the next major, the USPGA Championship which, lo and behold, he then went on to win by a street. If ever a death knell was sounded for wooden woods, it came with those two events.

The Early Days

And so a tradition stretching back over 500 years had come to a close. For ever since shepherds on the east coast of Scotland had used their crooks to propel stones across the expansive acres of St Andrews, and the seeds for the first claim on the game of golf had unwittingly been sewn, wood, glorious wood, had been the basic material used to enable stick to be laid on ball.

At any rate, that last bit is the story any Scotsman worth his salt would have you believe. Is it true that Scotland is the Home of Golf? In fact, the game's origins, like the origins of so many old sports, remain shrouded in mystery.

Did the Romans invent an early form of the sport when they came up with the game of *Pagancia*?

Only once in the Amateur Championship has a player won every single hole, thereby completing a ten and eight victory. The winner was an Irishman known as Captain Carter. Perhaps it is as well that the name of the vanquished American has been lost in the mists of time.

And what about the hybrids that came thereafter, as the Romans expanded their Empire, namely the pastime of *Jeu de mail* in Southern France and *cambuca* in England?

Then there is the Dutch game of *spel metten colve*, which means a game played with a club. By the thirteenth century it was well established and its name would evolve from colf to Kolf.

The thing that hampers all these arguments, however, is that none involved hitting a ball into a small hole and the Scots would like to point out – with good reason, to be fair – that this is, in fact, the whole *raison d'être* of the game.

As for how the game began in Scotland, one theory claims that fishermen, returning home from their boats, would pass the time by picking up a stick of driftwood and aiming a blow at a stone. In time perhaps a game developed between rival fishermen, the distance of competition stretching from boat to village or to the local hostelry. But when and how did the advent of the hole come about? Did a shepherd or fisherman hit upon the idea after a pebble finished in a rabbit scrape? We shall never be totally sure.

What is not in dispute is that the links at St Andrews would have been perfect for such a pursuit. And the Old Course there is appropriately named, for it is surely the oldest stretch of land in the world in continuous use for golf.

Golf had a hard time spreading the word for centuries. Though we know the game was being played in Scotland in the early 1400s, King James II hampered its development by banning it in

The nearest any player has come to completing the Grand Slam – the winning of the Open, the US Open, the Masters and the US PGA Championship in the same year – was Ben Hogan in 1953. He entered the first three and won them all. Indeed, so difficult is the task that only four players, Hogan, Jack Nicklaus, Gene Sarazen and Gary Player, have ever won all four titles during the course of their careers.

favour of archery practice in a Scottish Act of Parliament in 1457.

A century later, Mary Queen of Scots was so besotted by the game that she was back playing only a couple of days after the murder of her husband, Lord Darnley. Her action so appalled the Church that they issued her with a rebuke. So that was another black stain against golf's name.

Indeed so debilitating were setbacks like these that it would be another 200 years before the game's followers would get their act together sufficiently to develop a set of rules that achieved a broad consent.

Many people believe the Royal and Ancient Golf Club of St Andrews to be the oldest in the world but they are wrong. The R&A were beaten to the punch, as it were, by the Gentleman Golfers of Leith, later to be known, as they are today, as the Honourable Company of Edinburgh Golfers, whose modern home is that gem of a course just outside Scotland's capital city, Muirfield.

The Royal and Ancient, the game's governing body for everywhere outside America where it is controlled by the United States Golf Association, came into being ten years later. How did they get their name? They were known as the Society of St Andrews Golfers but the royal blessing was bestowed in 1834 by King William IV.

The first golf course in England was not established for another thirty years, when Old Tom Morris came down from St Andrews and laid out the links at Westward Ho! in Devon.

Perhaps no one has played better golf over a one-month stretch than Lee Trevino in the summer of 1971. In succession he won the US Open, the Canadian Open and the Open Championships.

If there is some dispute as to the origins of the game, there is none at all that the men in kilts were its pioneers. They took the sport to the world and the world loved them for it. It was largely through the efforts of Scottish traders that the game took hold on the eastern seaboard of America.

John Reid, an expatriate Scot from Dunfermline, Fife, is generally considered the 'father of American golf' on account of an epochal event on 22 February 1888. Gifted three woods and three irons that had been acquired for $2 each from Old Tom Morris at St Andrews by his schoolfriend Robert Lockhart, Reid, together with five other friends, crossed the road from his home into a nearby cow pasture. There they laid out America's first course – albeit one that had only three holes – and played the first 'round'. An exceptionally mild February allowed them to continue to play for a fortnight longer, before more typical weather brought the American golf revolution to a shuddering halt.

Reid, however, was deterred for only as long as it took the blizzards to clear. He bought a 30-acre site around the corner and spent a blissful summer with his friends developing his art. That November, after one round, they formed the St Andrew's Golf Club, distinguishing it from its Scottish predecessor by the use of the apostrophe. Reid was made president, his friend John Upham secretary and treasurer. Golf had officially arrived in the United States. And soon the trickle became a flood.

Records are there to be broken, they say, but two set by Byron Nelson in 1945 will stand for all time. During one remarkable run on the US Tour he won eleven tournaments in succession. His total number of victories for the season was an extraordinary eighteen.

Among the other early pioneers was Theodore Havermeyer, who was elected the first president of the United States Golf Association upon its formation in 1894. Six newly established clubs were present, including the Country Club of

Brookline and Shinnecock Hills. More than 100 years on, these two clubs still host the US Open; indeed, in 1999, the Country Club will stage the Ryder Cup.

It was not only to America that the Scots took the game. Similarly, trading links with India led to the establishment in 1829 of the Royal Calcutta Club, one of the oldest in the world. Golf came to the continent of Europe in 1856 when a group of visitors founded Pau in south-west France.

Africa had its pioneering clubs too, starting with Royal Cape in 1885, although the spread of the game to Australasia would not occur until the formation of Royal Christchurch in New Zealand in 1867. Oddly, the oldest club in Australia, the Royal Adelaide, only dates back to 1892 but there is evidence the game was played in the city as early as 1870.

The Golfing Boom

In golf there have been two great revolutions, the first encompassing the last thirty years of the nineteenth century and the second, broadly speaking, the same period in the twentieth.

It is always difficult to imagine a revolution while you are living through it, but even a cursory glance at life in the 1970s as compared to now illustrates the dramatic times we live in.

Total prize money in the Open Championship when Tom Watson won in 1977, for example, came to less than half of what the winner picked up just twenty years later. Similarly, the total prize money offered for everyone competing on the European

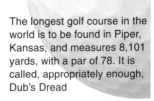

The longest golf course in the world is to be found in Piper, Kansas, and measures 8,101 yards, with a par of 78. It is called, appropriately enough, Dub's Dread.

Tour that year came to considerably less than what Colin Montgomerie collected on his own for his season's efforts in 1997.

The rise in the number of golf courses built has been similarly dramatic. In America it is estimated that 700 new courses are currently being built every year, and still they are struggling to keep up with demand.

One hundred years ago, the pace of change, relatively speaking, was equally bewildering. Although the first club in America was not formed until 1888, by the turn of the century more than 1,000 were in existence. In 1864, there were just 33 golf clubs in England and Scotland; by 1900 there were over 2,000.

Most of these were built south of the border. The Industrial Revolution had brought money to middle England and the dawn of the railway age gave them the facility to travel. Many imitated the Royal Family and journeyed to Scotland: when they returned their heads were filled with a love of a new game. Because it was the wealthy classes who were the first to travel, so they sought to keep the game to themselves when they returned. This primarily explains why the game has an elitist image in England, and, with son imitating father, why many older clubs have signs near the front entrance saying: 'Strictly private – members only'.

And so all over the UK, the newly developed seaside resorts set about building golf courses as a further attraction. Some of the great venues, like Turnberry, Royal Troon, and Royal Lytham, form part of the Victorian legacy. If you ever wondered why many of the great links courses have railway lines running parallel, here lies the answer.

Harry Vardon holds the record for the most Open Championship victories at six but he was less successful when it came to the matter of holes-in-one. Vardon, indeed, was coming towards the end of his life when he achieved his first ace. The odds against a hole-in-one for a top professional have been calculated at 3,700–1.

Changing Technology

Golf would never have become a working man's sport in Scotland but for the advent of the gutta percha ball. As the name suggests, it was made from gutta percha, a substance from the tropical percha tree that was found to be malleable when boiled in water, and so easily shaped into a ball. Furthermore, when it lost its shape or a piece had broken off, it could be reboiled and reshaped.

The gutta percha replaced the old feathery ball, which was expensive and easily damaged. The new missile cost a quarter of the price and lasted much longer.

It came into being in 1848 and played its part in the popularising of the sport. The guttie ball, as it became known, was king until the turn of the century when it was made redundant by the invention of the wound rubber-core Haskell ball.

The guttie ball had a revolutionary effect on golf club design. With the feathery ball, most clubs had had to be made of wood to minimise the damage. With the guttie, it was the clubs that suffered.

And so the slender, thin shape that had been dominant to that point began to disappear and in its place were clubs with heads that were shorter, broader and deeper. A brassie was introduced to the set, taking its name from the brass striking plate on the sole.

Then came the irons. Previously these had been used sparingly because of the harm they caused to the ball. But with the guttie the damage was minimal and their advantages became obvious. They were far cheaper to manufacture for a start.

Not surprisingly perhaps, St Andrews has hosted the Open Championship on more occasions than any other course. However it is only one ahead of Prestwick, which has not staged an Open since 1925. For the record St Andrews has hosted twenty-five Opens (the twenty-sixth will be in 2000) and Prestwick twenty-four.

By around 1900 most golf bags would contain seven or so irons, each with a different degree of loft: the driving cleek, iron cleek, lofter, mashie, sand iron, niblick and putting cleek.

Given the change in club head design, perhaps it was inevitable that the next development would see the demise of the hickory shaft. Maybe if the First World War had not come to dominate everything for almost a decade, they would have been used freely in the United States before the 1920s.

It was not until 1929, however, that the Royal and Ancient legalised them in Britain, and thereby hangs a tale. Imagine the commotion there must have been when the Prince of Wales (the future Edward VII) turned up for a competition at the Old Course at St Andrews and proceeded to the first tee using a set of clubs with steel shafts?

How thoroughly radical and decidedly un-royal. It is said that the Prince's actions forced the R&A's hands: to make steel shafts legal or disqualify the Prince? Guess which action they chose?

Mass-produced clubs quickly followed the decision to legalise and so too did the use of numbers for irons rather than names. Soon there were so many clubs on the market that the wealthy would take to the course with twenty or more implements, which must have been hell for the caddy.

In the semi-finals of the 1997 Dunhill Cup, Joakim Haeggman, representing Sweden, went to the turn at St Andrews in just twenty-seven strokes. It equalled the lowest nine-hole score achieved anywhere. Asked about Haeggman's performance, his playing partner Justin Leonard noted: 'All I said was "good shot", "nice drive", "no, you're still on the tee". I made sure I kept the card real neat because I knew it was going on a wall somewhere.'

The ruling authorities duly took pity on them. On 1 January 1938, the USGA imposed the fourteen-club limit rule which stands today – the R&A followed a year later – 'to restore the making of individual shots and increase the skill of the player'.

It is enough to make any self-respecting greenkeeper recoil in horror. Using his precious green as a teeing ground to drive for the next hole? Yet this was the practice during the game's formative years, before being abandoned in favour of separate teeing grounds, which not only saved the greens from wear and tear but also speeded up play.

Until the early 1900s and the arrival of celluloid tees, players used a small mould of sand for the purpose. Each tee would have a sand box, which would be refilled each morning by the greenkeeper.

Gradually, the practicality of plastic or wooden tees became obvious. Today the only boxes alongside teeing grounds are generally of the litter collecting variety.

Balls

The entrepreneurs not only made their contribution in the field of golf club development. There was the ball as well, and setting things in motion, so to speak, was a wealthy American amateur called Coburn Haskell and his collaborator Bertram Work, an engineer with the Goodrich Rubber Company in Ohio.

They believed that the guttie had reached its limitations. Rubber was cheap and plentiful and their idea was to wind lengths of it around a solid core, the inevitable 'spring' bringing about dramatic differences in how far the ball could be struck.

The benefits, however, were not apparent at first, as the early prototypes dived and curved. For once, golfers were right to blame their equipment for hooks and slices!

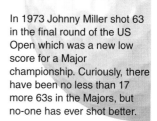

In 1973 Johnny Miller shot 63 in the final round of the US Open which was a new low score for a Major championship. Curiously, there have been no less than 17 more 63s in the Majors, but no-one has ever shot better.

Haskell and Work, however, were not to be deterred. The creation of an automatic winding machine, together with a different cover with raised bumps, produced significantly improved results.

The Haskell ball was used by its maker from 1898, and was introduced commercially at the dawn of the new century. It did not take long for its qualities to become clear. Walter J. Travis won the US Amateur Championship in 1901 using the Haskell. The following year, across the Atlantic, Sandy Herd won the Open, also using the Haskell.

Golfers have never been slow to gorge upon a new development. The Haskell quickly became the ball of choice and led to a surge in experimentation over the next twenty years as other manufacturers tried different materials for the cores and covers.

By 1920 golfers could choose between 200 different golf balls, at which point the ruling authorities stepped in to decide on a uniform ball that had to be 1.62 inches in diameter.

Ten years later the United States Golf Association increased this to 1.68 inches, and for sixty years players outside the US had a choice that was denied when playing in America.

The bigger ball had both pros and cons. It did not travel so far and was more difficult to control in the wind. Hence at the Open, which invariably would be played in anything from a zephyr to a gale, all the players would switch willingly to the smaller ball. Yet for the better player the bigger variation offered more feel and was easier to use on the greens.

By the 1980s the improvements in both club and

A fifty-nine is a figure with a mythical status in golf, rather like the four-minute mile in athletics. But whereas once the four-minute mile was breached everyone seemed to beat it, in golf a 59 has remained an almost impossible figure. It was first achieved in 1959 by Sam Snead; only Al Geiberger and Chip Beck have since emulated his feat.

ball technology meant that the pros had far outweighed the cons. The wind factor had ceased to be so relevant. The smaller ball had outlived its use and in 1990 the Royal and Ancient recognised this by making the American ball size mandatory worldwide.

Frankly, it is a good job they did. If Tiger Woods was using a small ball now there is little doubt that he would be able to drive it 400 yards every time he teed it up.

More Balls

You would think that there would be a limited amount that you could do with a golf ball wouldn't you? Once the size had been decided upon, its insides, that dimples were far better than bumps when it came to accentuating lift and minimising drag, that balata was an ideal substance for a cover ... what else could there be for heaven's sake?

Well, until new technology came along, not a lot. Golf balls were white and if you thinned one on a frosty November morning you knew that your hands would sting and you also knew it was time to burrow in your golf bag and fetch out another one.

You could say times have changed. Now there are 1,500 golf balls approved by the United States Golf Association and they are made by over 100 different companies. Well over two million balls are manufactured each day in America alone.

Balls to help you hit it high. Balls to help you hit it low. Balls that alleviate a hook or slice. Balls that enable a player to impart so much spin that it

With 18 Major championship titles Jack Nicklaus is well ahead of Walter Hagen's 11 in the all-time winners list. but perhaps even more remarkable than his triumphs has been Nicklaus's overall record. He has, for example, finished in the top five in no less than 56 Majors, and his top ten showing at the 1998 Masters was his 72nd top ten finish – a nice golfing number for the ultimate professional golfer.

appears he is talking to it. Balls with 332 dimples. Balls with 500 dimples. Balls with dimples in shapes that go by names that are impossible to pronounce. Balls with lithium-sodium-zinc covers. Balls with surlyn-balata covers. Pink balls. Yellow balls. Logoed balls.

Even those in the industry concede that they have failed the public by producing such a vast amount of, well, balls.

'We have confused the public by having so many products on the market', a spokesman at Maxfli admitted when I visited their factory in South Carolina a couple of years ago. 'Many golfers have switched off and stick by the same belief that they always had; that a golf ball is a golf ball is a golf ball.' How quaint.

It was not only the equipment directly used in playing golf that developed as the twentieth century wore on. So did the secondary items as well, such as the golf bag.

Prior to their introduction in the late 1890s, players used to carry their clubs in a bundle under their arms – or rather a caddy did. The early golf bags generally consisted of a wooden tripod supporting a slim canvas tube.

Today golf bags have more pockets than a pair of army trousers. A top professional's bag will weigh around 35lbs and contain everything that he could possibly require on the course, from a couple of bananas to a pack of elastoplast.

With his victory at the 1997 Masters Tiger Woods created a slew of records in his first Major championship as a professional. Perhaps the pick of these was his winning 12-stroke margin which was an achievement unequalled this century. He also became the youngest winner of the Masters and his winning total of 270 broke the old 72 hole Augusta record by a stroke.

Clubs

If 1,500 different types of golf ball were not enough to contend with, what about clubs? Here again the manufacturers have gone for quantity. There is not a manufacturer anywhere who does not bring out a new club every year.

Of course, they all come up with the same hyperbole. Revolutionary design ... minimises bad shots ... increases distance ... heck, if every club was that much of an improvement on the previous model, the average golfer would by now be going around in 55 not 85.

What has been startling are the changes in the names of the manufacturers themselves. The idea that golfers, if they are happy with one make of clubs, will settle for that manufacturer next time, thereby exhibiting the same sort of brand loyalty that frequently happens when, say, buying a new car, is fanciful.

Ten years ago no golf magazine carried a single advert for Callaway, and very few for Taylor Made. Now the former is the world's biggest club manufacturer and the latter the fastest growing.

You could say that marketing has proved everything here, and these manufacturers have certainly cornered the market of modern golfers, who change their clubs more often. But equally they appeal to the established player as well these days. The bottom line is their products are good – and word of mouth has done the rest.

The first time prize money was offered at the Open championship was in 1864 when Tom Morris received £6 for first prize. In 1998, the winner of the Open walked off with a cheque for £300,000.

Best of all, they have even persuaded people to part with £400 or more for a single golf club. Brilliant!

Courses

So everyone is happy, yes? Improvements to clubs and balls mean that someone aged fifty-five can still hit the ball the same distance as when he or she was thirty-five. Furthermore, the condition of golf courses has improved out of all recognition over the last twenty years. Those of you who are new to the sport and simply love golf on television must think it is an easy game played on unfailingly beautiful venues.

So why am I not happy with all these 'improvements?' Why are many traditionalists not happy?

Because they have changed the way that golf courses are built. And they have also rendered many of the old masterpieces obsolete. Merion for example, in America. This was one of the great sites for the US Open but, at 6,700 yards long, it has not held one since 1981 because it is too short to cope with golf clubs brandishing names like Great Big Bertha.

Then there is Augusta, which still looks idyllic and still captures the imagination every Spring. But the event you watch every April hardly compares to the one that hosted the tournament in the 1950s, and for the evidence it is instructive to compare the way that Ben Hogan played the eleventh hole during that decade and how Tiger Woods played it in 1997.

Hogan wrote: 'I always considered the 11th a brute of a par four, and my strategy was to play to the right of the green with my long iron approach and then chip down to the putting surface, thereby taking the water that protects the green out of play. Believe me, anytime I was on that green in two, it meant that I had mishit my second shot.'

Woods did not need a long iron for his second shot, he hit a sand wedge. Over the back. Woods did not worry about the water, which is such a fundamental part of the hole's armoury. No professional worries about water with a sand wedge in his hands.

And so it went on. Woods did not need more than a nine iron for his second shot to any par four in seventy-two holes. The par fives were more about which iron to choose to play for the second shot. As it turned out, the most he needed was a four iron.

What is the solution? To date, the answer seems to have been to build golf courses that are displeasing to the eye and depressing to play. Two of the most famous holes in world golf are the seventh at Pebble Beach and the Postage Stamp at Troon. Together they do not measure 250 yards; two short holes that test every golfer's skill and bring a shiver of anticipation every time a player stands on the tee.

But where is their equivalent today? A par three measuring 120 yards, par fours under 300 yards, have become an anachronism. Far too many modern courses feature a succession of holes measuring 450 yards par four, and the game is the poorer for it. Brute force has replaced gentle imagination. Too many new courses have been built with merely professional golf in mind, totally forgetting that the average male handicap in Britain is twenty not two. Get a top tournament, get exposure, and the people will surely flock in its wake.

This is the strategy and it is probably true. But the only golf course in the UK that has been built adopting this course of action that actually looks good on television and I would run to play is Loch Lomond.

The Five Grand Masters

Harry Vardon: Three players dominated golf at the beginning of the twentieth century and they became known as the Great Triumvirate. Vardon was the greatest of the Great.

His record of six Open Championships has still to be equalled. He also won the US Open for good measure.

Vardon's reign at the top came at a time when there were very few tournaments and so consequently he topped up his income with a series of money matches and exhibitions.

In so doing he spread the word of golf, as people came from miles around to watch. At the height of his powers, he spent a year in America playing such matches and was beaten only twice.

In 1903 he was struck down by tuberculosis and never really recovered, although he was to win the Open twice more.

But with his illness came human frailty, and he became the first prominent player to suffer from the 'yips'. There would be many more.

Francis Ouimet: Francis Ouimet's victory in the 1913 US Open changed the course of American golf. The triumph of a twenty-year-old from an ordinary family inspired the whole country. A game perceived as belonging to the wealthy was now taken up by all.

Ouimet might not have come from rich stock, but he was fortunate to have been brought up in a house

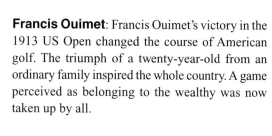

in Brookline, Massachusetts, that was but a stone's throw from the Country Club.

He was a caddy there from the age of eleven, and permitted to play the course. Nine years later it was simply enough for him to be teeing it up alongside the best professionals of the day when the US Open came to his home course.

With six holes to play in the final round, though, Ouimet was two strokes adrift of Harry Vardon and Ted Ray and heading for an honourable third place. He then exceeded even his wildest dreams by finishing with two birdies and winning the play-off.

In 1951 he became the first American golfer to be elected captain of the Royal and Ancient. The Country Club, incidentally, will host the 1999 Ryder Cup.

Gene Sarazen: Gene Sarazen remains one of only four players to have won all four major championships at least once. Perhaps the most famous of all his triumphs came in the 1935 Masters, when he holed his second shot to the par five 15th for an albatross.

The full-blooded four wood vaulted him from nowhere to a tie with Craig Wood and he won the play-off. It became known as the 'shot heard around the world' and it helped make Augusta famous.

It was around the time of his Masters triumph that Sarazen thought hard about improving his bunker play. He decided it was the tools that were to blame and set about building one with a heavy sole, which could cut through the sand. The Sarazen sand iron became the forerunner of the club we use today.

Well into his nineties, Sarazen mixed with the modern professionals and saluted how they had improved his craft. There was no resentment at the money they earned, the skill they showed. At the 1993 Open he stood wide-eyed by the 18th green as Greg Norman holed out for a 64 to win. 'I never thought I would live to see golf played like this', he said.

Arnold Palmer: Golf in the 1950s was a grey sport. The best player was Ben Hogan and while he held those interested in the game in thrall he appealed to no one outside its narrow boundaries. Then came Arnold Palmer. He appeared at a time when colour television had started to replace black and white: his effect on golf was rather similar.

Here was handsome Palmer, with cool hairstyle and cool cigarette hanging out of the corner of his mouth, demolishing the careful strategy espoused by Hogan and others in the 1950s. Palmer's strategy was smash it, find it, and smash it again.

He electrified everyone, not only inside golf but outside it as well. Instead of a polite crowd of a few hundred we had the rowdy thousands known as Arnie's Army.

For a while they were unstoppable and so was the man himself. From 1958 to 1964 he won no less than seven major championships. Palmer turned up at the Open and revolutionised an event that was in danger of losing its status.

Even meeting him for the first time when he was

well into middle age, one could not help but be affected by his charisma. He also gave the best press conference I have ever seen: a moving farewell to the US Open at his beloved Oakmont in 1994.

'It's not as if I have won very much', he said and then just broke down and sobbed. But golf was always about so much more than winning and no man ever did better in this regard than Palmer.

Jack Nicklaus: To say that early in his career Jack Nicklaus was Darth Vader to Arnold Palmer's Han Solo is to underestimate how much he was disliked by the golfing galleries. When challenging Palmer one year for the US Open, the then chubby Nicklaus spied a banner in the heavy rough, which read: 'Put your ball here, fat boy.'

That Nicklaus was able to overcome such hostility and to win them over until they loved him almost as much as Palmer himself is testament not only to his golf but to the development of his personality.

Fat boy became ideally built man and dominated golf like no man had done before. When he had finished he had won eighteen major championships: to put that total in its true context, no one else has won more than eleven.

Nicklaus has not only rewritten the record book but the one on sportsmanship as well. In 1969 he conceded a 3ft putt to Tony Jacklin which meant a halved Ryder Cup match. 'I don't think you would have missed it, but I was not prepared to let you try', Nicklaus told him.

The Golden Bear not only won more majors than anyone else, he also finished second more than anyone else. Each time he did so with a dignity that made him the perfect ambassador for his sport.

His legacy is seen in the behaviour of the men who thought of him as a role model. Players like Greg Norman, whose grace under pressure after throwing away the 1996 Masters earned him more plaudits than if he had won.

COMPETITION										Please indicate which tee used		
										PAR SSS	73 74	
Date		Time		Entry No.			Handicaps	Strokes rec'd				
Player A										PAR SSS	73 73	
Player B										PAR SSS	72 72	
Marker's score	Hole	White yards	Par	Yellow yards	Stroke Index	Score A	B	Nett score	W = + L = - H = 0	Red yards	Par	Stroke Index
	1	471	5	462	9					425	5	9
	2	155	3	137	17					121	3	17
	3	452	4	447	3					376	4	1
	4	501	5	479	11					421	5	13
	5	191	3	167	15					143	3	16
	6	356	4	328	13					310	4	11
	7	399	4	362	5					333	4	7
	8	398	4	389	7					346	4	3
	9	450	4	435	1					423	5	5
	OUT	3373	36	3206						2898	37	

P L E A S E   A V O I D   S L O W   P L A Y   A T   A L L   T I M E S

	10	186	3	177	10					174	3	14
	11	376	4	371	6					318	4	4
	12	483	5	468	14					448	5	10
	13	441	4	423	2					400	5	15
	14	179	3	179	18					117	3	18
	15	466	4	458	4					405	4	2
	16	380	4	369	16					352	4	12
	17	571	5	538	8					474	5	6
	18	502	5	486	12					458	5	8
	IN	3584	37	3469						3146	38	
	OUT	3373	36	3206						2898	37	
	TOTAL	6957	73	6675						6044	75	
		STABLEFORD POINTS OR NETT RESULT	HANDICAP							Holes won		
			NETT							Holes lost		
Marker's signature				Player's signature						Result		

A typical golf card, in this case for the West Course at Wentworth

Golf is the only major sport where the rules are not there to be interpreted or bullied, where a player does not strive to see what he can get away with. In golf there is no equivalent to a referee adjudging whether a player has dived or not in the penalty area; no umpire to decide, for instance, whether a ball was caught before it touched the ground.

In short, and outside professional tournaments, there is no one to whom a player can appeal to claim his innocence. The sole arbiter is the professional himself and while in theory that appears a cheat's charter, in practice it is just the opposite.

For cheating in golf is not so much frowned upon as the moment when all hell is let loose. The rules are dyed on the hearts of all who love the sport and passed from father to son, mother to daughter, friend to friend. Commit adultery if he must; live off immoral earnings if necessary; sell his daughter into slavery; but, heavens, no player, no professional, must cheat.

There is the famous story of a solicitor in Leicestershire who did cheat, nudging his ball into a better lie in the rough. He was caught, and thrown out of his club. Worse, he found his business went to pot, as his customers deserted him in droves. The clients believed that if their solicitor could cheat at golf he could cheat at anything and so was not to be trusted with their business.

When the amateur David Robertson was caught cheating he was banned from entering competitions for ten years. Ten years! What would you have to do in football or cricket to be banned for that length of time? Probably murder an official.

The message is clear then: a professional must learn the rules. And here we enter a problematical area. For have you ever seen the golf rules book? Ever picked it up, tried to read it? It is a bible for insomniacs. How boring is it? Well put it this way. Cheating, as we now know, is by far the worst sin that anyone can commit on a golf course – and yet every week a professional somewhere inadvertently breaks the regulations because better that than wading through and learning the rules book.

And so a codicil has to be added to the earlier statement about golfers having the rules of the game dyed on their hearts: what is dyed there is the spirit of the rules of the game, one based on Tom Watson's theory, which reads: 'When you strip the game down to the bare essentials there are only two basic rules that matter. One, play the ball as it lies. Two, if you do not know what to do next, do what you think is fair.'

It is a sound philosophy, one that would enable a golfer to come to terms with many situations on a golf course. All the same it is sad that many more players do not learn the regulations. Are they really that obtuse?

Sadly, yes. If the Plain English Society ever got hold of the rules book they would have a field day. For example: let's see, just open the book here at random and what do we find, ah yes, rule 26-1, Ball in Water Hazard. 'It is a question of fact whether a ball lost after having been struck toward a water hazard is lost inside or outside the hazard. In order to treat the ball as lost in the hazard, there must be reasonable evidence that the ball lodged in it.'

Now is it me, or are these two contradictory

Putting: To the novice golfer it must seem a curious practice. A professional locates the green with his approach shot and then whips off the glove that covers his right hand and places it neatly in his back pocket. All a bit pretentious, what? Actually no. People can go on about great technique when it comes to putting but the vital ingredient that enables a player to hole a number of putts is a sense of feel. And the sense of feel has to be greater with both hands on the grip of the putter.

sentences? On the one hand it is a question of fact. On the other it is reasonable evidence.

Not only are the rules badly written, they are complex as well. There are only 34 rules in golf but there are so many sub-clauses, indexes, amendments, and appendices, that it feels more like 34,000. Actually, throw in the books dealing with the decisions on the rules of golf, and there *are* 34,000.

As for the basic rules themselves, there is not only Rule 25, for example, but Rule 25-1, Rule 25-1 a,b,c, not to mention Rule 25-1 c (i), oh and not forgetting Rule 25-1 c (i) (a), (b), and (c). Confused? Of course. Who would not be?

Incidentally, this last one is a beauty. Rule 25-1 c (i) reads: 'Outside a Hazard: If a ball is lost outside a hazard under a condition covered by Rule 25-1, the player may take relief as follows: the point on the course nearest to where the ball last crossed the margin of the area shall be determined which (a) is not nearer the hole than where the ball last crossed the margin, (b) avoids interference by the condition and (c) is not in a hazard or on a putting green. He shall drop a ball without penalty within one club length of the point thus determined on a part of the course which fulfils (a), (b), and (c) above'.

Got all that? Thought not. At least you're in good company.

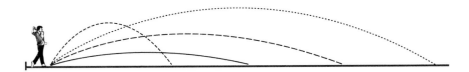

The Early Rules

It was all so simple way back when. The first rules of golf were drawn up just over 250 years ago and there were only 13 of them. No clauses, no sub-clauses, and certainly no indexes or appendices.

I like Rule V the best: 'If your ball come among Watter, or any Wattery filth, you are at liberty to take out your Ball and throw it behind the hazard, six yards at least; you may play it with any club, and allow your Adversary a stroke or so for getting out your Ball.'

The trouble was that these rules only covered the general aspects of matchplay. There was no provision for a lost ball or out of bounds, for example. As the game evolved, so did the complexity of the rules. By 1812 we were up to 17 rules, drawn up by the St Andrews Society of Golfers.

The cut: After two rounds of every 72-hole tournament a cut is made, whereby the first 70 players and ties progress to complete the event and the rest of the field goes home. The figure of 70 is not arbitrary. In the Masters, which has a much smaller starting field – usually around 90, as against as many as 156 in a regular tour event – only 44 move on to the final 36 holes. Also, in any of the four major championships, anyone within ten shots of the lead plays on.

By 1888, the game was in a chaotic state, with no clear code as to how it should be played. Clubs made up rules to suit their own terrain. If you lost a ball at St Andrews, for example, the punishment was loss of hole. At Hoylake, however, you had to return to the place where you played the shot and lose a stroke in addition. At Bembridge you struck another near where you lost the ball and added two strokes.

It was in 1897 that St Andrews was accepted as the game's arbitrary authority. Incidentally, of the options before them regarding loss of a ball: their own punishment was considered too harsh, as was Bembridge's; golf has proceeded ever since using the Hoylake principle.

In 1997, therefore, the Rules of Golf committee celebrated their centenary, and, contrary to popular opinion, the personnel have changed once or twice during the period. In that time, they have handed out literally hundreds of thousands of judgements to people who have written in with queries.

When you see some of the questions, you realise why the rules have clauses and sub-clauses, as they try to cover every eventuality.

One golfer wrote in to ask what he was supposed to do in the following bizarre circumstances: 'I hooked my second shot towards a teeing area where a golfer was driving off and inadvertently he missed his ball and struck mine back flush towards me. What happens next?'

What should have happened next is the letter writer play his ball from where it lies while the unfortunate soul teeing off would incur no penalty but the stroke would count.

Sometimes it is not a judgement that is asked for but clairvoyancy. One lady wrote to the R&A explaining that she would not bore the committee with the facts but could they possibly help her concerning a match which she had won at the seventeenth but lost at the twenty-first?

A man asked the committee to settle an argument that was dividing his club. He related the case and then concluded by saying that if the committee did not agree with him they need not bother replying.

The R&A were appointed the arbiters of the rules of golf only on condition that clubs were allowed to set their own by-laws that were peculiar to that course.

Thus, it has become perfectly allowable to move golf balls away from alligators if one's ball finishes near them in Florida or South Carolina. And in the years after the last war, there was no need to play a ball that had finished close to an unexploded shell – why, one could move it without suffering a penalty.

My favourite, though, is a local rule at the Nyanza club in Africa. It reads: 'If a ball comes to rest in dangerous proximity to a hippopotamus or crocodile, another ball may be dropped at a safe distance, no nearer the hole, without penalty.'

Gee, thanks a bunch.

Professional Errors

Golf is the only major professional sport where the act itself is not enough. If it was, then Roberto de Vicenzo would have been in a play-off for the 1968 Masters. After all, millions of television viewers saw the Argentine birdie the 17th in the final round and so post a score that was exactly the same as Bob Goalby's.

But de Vicenzo marked down a four instead of a three and, under the rules, the higher score had to stand. He lost the Masters on a card infringement and with it the chance of a million dollars in endorsements.

Because they are not sticklers for the rules, and they don't know every clause and sub-clause by heart, tens of thousands of pounds are tossed away each year by professionals through disqualifications caused by ignorance.

This is despite the fact you will often see play

Pin position: The location of the hole on each green will change every day during a tournament. Clearly, on every green there is the potential to choose difficult pin positions – behind a bunker, for example – or an easy one, say in the middle of the putting surface, or one between these two extremes. Most greenkeepers will usually opt for six of each variety during a round, unless the course is easy and the professionals are scoring low, in which case there will be more difficult ones than ever.

interrupted as they seek out a ruling from tour referees. So petrified are they of making a mistake that they place the burden on another's shoulders.

Even so the errors occur, usually when the pressure is on and a player's mind is elsewhere. In 1997, a simple rules infraction at the Players' Championship cost Davis Love a six-figure payday.

Nick Faldo has built his reputation on being the most meticulous of golfers, leaving nothing to chance. Yet at least three times in his career he has found himself on the wrong side of the line as far as the rules are concerned.

The most recent occured in the 1994 Open at Turnberry when he charged into heavy rough after his ball and charged out again after playing it. The problem lay in the fact that he had given the ball only the most cursory of glances and, when he reached the fairway, discovered to his horror that it was not his. The result of this act of carelessness was a two-stroke penalty.

Ernie Els concentrates on checking his card

In this television age, players also have to watch what they say. At one tournament Tom Watson and Lee Trevino were walking to a tee and a television microphone picked up the former telling the latter how to cure a fault. A viewer phoned in to say Watson was in breach of the rules, because he was giving advice. The complaint was upheld and Watson was penalised.

In 1992 Mike McLean was challenging hard for the Dutch Open when he drove into trees over the closing holes. Behind his ball was a piece of vine and McLean moved it out of the way. Unfortunately for the Kent golfer the vine was still attached to its roots and therefore should not have been moved. The two-stroke penalty cost him the title.

Even more cruel was the fate that befell Martin Poxon at the final event of the 1993 season, the Madrid Open. At the time Poxon lay 125th in the order of merit and needed to make up five places to keep his card to play in events the following year. An opening 69 was just the start he was looking for.

At the 17th in the second round, however, Poxon's ball finished in a pool of water on the green and, finding the nearest point of relief off the green, he dropped there. Under the rules, however, he should have placed the ball, because the ball had previously been on the green. Ironically, because preferred lies (*see Glossary*) were in operation, this is what he ended up doing after he had dropped it.

Because the error only came to light after he had signed for his card, the resultant two-shot penalty meant that he had to be disqualified.

Watson's twin beliefs about golf, either to play it as it lies or do what you think is fair, did not help poor Poxon much.

And the rule in question? Why our old friend, Rule 25-1 b (iii). There, I told you that you were not the only one confused by 25-1 and its sub-clauses.

The professional, it seems, will always be prone to catastrophes befalling them, but John Paramor, Director of Tour Operations in Europe and Chief Referee, remains unsympathetic.

Left to right putt: A lot of greens are built with contours and consequently, on a lot of putts, there is more to it than simply aiming at the hole. A left to right putt comes about when the ball has to go over land that is falling towards the hole; the player has to compensate by aiming for the left of the cup, for the ball will move during its motion to the right.

'The whole process of this game is that the players are supposed to know the rules as they have to regulate themselves', he argues. 'That is effectively the ethos of the game, and the rules make no allowance for ignorance. You should always know the rules of your chosen game.

'We are the shop window for the game and we have a mission to set an example to everyone who plays it. We all want to see people excel at a sport we play ourselves, but we want to know they are playing under the same rules of golf as we do in the monthly medal.

'Players have access to us at all times on the course because the marshals can contact us via radio. What we are trying to do is to educate the players in the rules.'

Paramor never ceases to be amazed at the level of ignorance shown by some of the top players. 'I remember watching Seve Ballesteros at the 1995 World Matchplay Championship and I could not believe my eyes. One of the most experienced competitors committed two basic breaches because he was not thinking. Firstly he removed an imbedded acorn from the line of his putt when you are only allowed to move loose impediments, and then he tapped down the indentation with his putter when you are only allowed to tap down pitch marks.

'I went to see Seve about it and he was fine, accepting it completely. He said he should have known better.'

One player who would sympathise was Davis Love. As the son of a professional he is steeped in the

Seve Ballesteros

game and believes he knows the rules. 'But once you put your competitive hat on you are concentrating so hard that you simply forget about some of the other stuff', he contended.

That probably explains many of the seemingly basic errors that professionals make. All the same, the pressure of competition is only part of the reason. Adherence to the rules is one area where many amateurs could educate the professionals.

Basic Rules to Enhance your Viewing Pleasure

Rule 7: Practice

Practice is not permitted on the golf course before a strokeplay competition. Before the start of each round every caddy is handed a sheet informing him where the pins will be placed on the greens for that day.

If their employers are doing well, many caddies will walk the course in the morning, to see how the ball reacts when it pitches on a certain green. Say a flag has been tucked behind a bunker. The caddy wants to ascertain whether his player can get the ball to stop if he plays aggressively towards the flag.

Over borrowed: Take, for a moment, the putt previously mentioned. If a player aims too far to the left and the ball does not swing down far enough and passes the hole on the left, he has over borrowed. If he has not borrowed enough, the ball will pass the hole on the right.

No player is allowed to practise a putt before he steps up to hit it in competition. He is, however, allowed to replay the shot again should he choose, although it is the first effort that counts on the scorecard. You will also see all players carefully study the putts of their playing partners, guaging the pace and the severity of the contour before they take their putts.

Rule 8: Advice

I'm going to let you into a little trade secret here. Players bend the law all the time when it comes to rule eight. The regulation states that no advice can be asked for or given between players, which means that if a player hits the ball next to the pin at a short hole, his playing partner cannot ask him what club he played. Yet the players get round this stipulation all the time. They have unspoken rules. They might peer in their playing partner's bag, for example, and work out which iron he played by the one that is missing. Or the caddie might take a little longer cleaning the blade, giving the other player plenty of time to see what number was written on the bottom of the club.

Off the course, players give each other advice all the time, which is perfectly legal. On the practice ground you will often see players passing on their wisdom, telling their friends where they believe they are going wrong. Some refugees from other sports might consider this rather strange behaviour – why would they give advice to people whom they are trying to defeat? – but players have never looked upon other players as their opponents. It is the golf course they are attempting to flatten.

Rule 10: Order of Play

On the first tee in competition the player who drives first is the one whose name appeared first on the ballot sheet. Thereafter, the player who drives the shortest distance will play his second shot first and then the next shortest and so on. This continues until the hole is finished. The player who records the lowest score on the hole will tee off first on the next hole, or 'have the honour' as it is termed.

It is against the rules of golf to ground a club in a bunker before playing the shot.

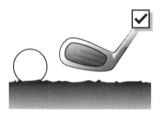

Swing Thought: A golf swing is over so quickly that much of it is completed by habit. However, there is time enough to have one swing thought, and so most players will think of one thing that enables every other thing to hopefully fall into place. It may be a very simple thought: Nick Faldo, for example, recently thought of nothing more than keeping his head over the ball long after putts had been struck. What invariably leads to chaos is trying to have two swing thoughts: the hands and the brain cannot cope.

There is no penalty for breaking this code in strokeplay competition. In matchplay competition however, such as the Ryder Cup, it is entirely within the rules for one side to ask the other to play a shot again if it is deemed that an advantage is gained by playing out of turn.

Rule 13: Ball Played as it Lies

From the moment the ball leaves the tee to when it disappears into the hole, it must be played as it lies. Of course, this being the rules of golf, nothing is that straightforward – there are exceptions. One is if there has been a tempest and the tournament director deems that the fairways are so soft that there is a strong likelihood that the balls will plug upon landing; in which case, 'preferred lies' come into operation. Preferred lies enable a player to pick up his ball and clean it, replacing it within six inches of where it landed but no nearer the hole.

Another exception is if the ball finishes in a water hazard or is unplayable through some other means (we'll come to the options in these instances shortly).

If a ball finishes in the trees no branches may be broken or bent in order to make a decent swing at the ball. The only things that are allowed to be moved are loose objects, such as twigs, leaves, or acorns, but only if they result in the ball not moving. If it does move, the golfer is penalised two shots.

In a bunker a player is not allowed to touch the sand with his club while addressing the ball, and if it happens to have finished in its own imprint then that is just plain bad luck. A player is not permitted to smooth out the sand behind the ball.

Rules 16 and 17: The Putting Green

The player is on the green and the flag is in the hole. If he sinks the putt, he will suffer a two-stroke penalty as he has hit the pin.

He is now off the green and is either putting or chipping to the hole. If the ball goes in, he is not penalised. The short grass around the green counts as fairway in this case.

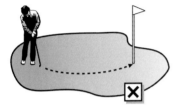

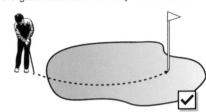

His partner is holding the flag, as the ball is some way from the pin and the hole would otherwise be difficult to see properly.

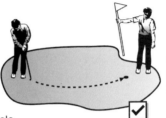

When the player hits the ball, the partner removes the pin.

The player can see the hole without the pin in place. The pin is removed and placed on the green before the putt.

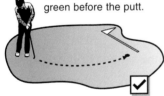

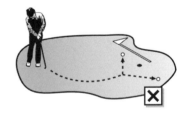

Except when preferred lies are in operation, the only time a player is allowed to pick up a ball and clean it is when it is on the putting green, when both can be done without penalty. All players will use a ball marker or a lucky coin to mark where the ball lay and they are completely precise in this matter. Replacing the ball one inch to the side of the coin is not acceptable.

Normally players mark their balls on the green with a marker. If this is not done and the putter hits another ball with his, there is a two-stroke penalty to the non-putting player.

The Drop
The arm must be extended
straight, parallel to the ground.

Texas wedge: This has
always referred to the
practice of using a putter
from off the green.
However, in more recent
times, its scope has been
widened. Now it is often
used to describe the way
players use a driver or
three wood as a putter
when the ball has come to
rest up against a fringe of
rough just off the green.

When he is studying the line of a putt, you may
see a player sweep away some small stones that
have strayed from a bunker, or leaves, or a
pitchmark left by some other golfer. All these
things they are allowed to do. They are not
allowed, however, to pat down spike marks that
may litter their path. That is why most players
prefer to play early in the morning, before the
greens have had to cope with much traffic.

While putting, a player can either have the flag
out or attended by his caddy, who will remove
it before the ball reaches the hole. What he is
not allowed to do is have the flag left in
unattended. A ball striking it in this manner
would result in a two-stroke penalty. There is
no penalty, however, for striking the flag while
off the green.

Rule 26: Water Hazards

A water hazard is any sea, lake, ditch, pond, river
or other open water course – whether containing
water or not – and will be defined by yellow
stakes. A lateral water hazard is one where it is
deemed impractical to drop the ball behind the
said hazard, and will be defined by red stakes.

If a ball goes into a water hazard, a player will
drop behind it under penalty of one stroke in line
with the point of entry. A player has to be sure it
entered the hazard, either through seeing it splash
down or the tell-tale ripple signs. Otherwise it must
be treated as a lost ball.

A lost ball means replaying the shot from as near
as possible to the original spot, again adding a one-
stroke penalty.

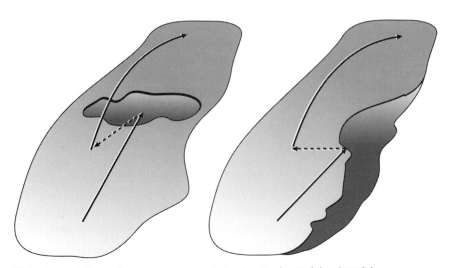

Water hazard. The ball must be dropped behind the point of entry and a one-shot penalty incurred.

Lateral water hazard, ie where it is impossible to drop a ball behind the hazard. The ball must be dropped at the point of entry and a one-stroke penalty incurred.

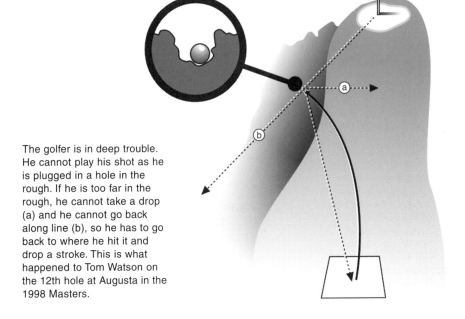

The golfer is in deep trouble. He cannot play his shot as he is plugged in a hole in the rough. If he is too far in the rough, he cannot take a drop (a) and he cannot go back along line (b), so he has to go back to where he hit it and drop a stroke. This is what happened to Tom Watson on the 12th hole at Augusta in the 1998 Masters.

If the ball entered a lateral water hazard, once more a shot will be added and replayed from a point within two club lengths of where the ball entered the hazard.

Rule 27: Ball Lost or Out of Bounds

A lost ball is a decidedly rare occurrence in professional golf for not only are there spectators around to point out to a player where it has landed in the rough but usually marshalls as well. Nevertheless, it still happens that a player will not walk straight to his ball and, in that instance, he is allowed five minutes to search; if it is not found he has to return from whence he came and replay the shot, under penalty of a stroke. If he has hit a shot into a pile of trouble and it is clear he may be looking for his ball for some time, he is allowed to play a 'provisional' ball, in case the original can not be found.

A ball is out of bounds if it is wholly beyond any boundary fence gully, or other area usually determined by white posts. Any other out-of-bounds delineations will normally be marked under the local rules of a club.

Rule 28: Ball Unplayable

A player may declare his ball unplayable at any point on the course, except when it is in the confines of a water hazard, when rule 26 applies. He has three options. Adding a penalty of one stroke, he may either: drop the ball from shoulder height within two club lengths of where the ball lies, though not nearer the hole; drop the ball behind the point where it lay while keeping the trouble between himself and the hole with no limit

Drop zone: These are often used in professional tournaments. Around many holes the stands are situated close to a green and a wayward shot can often end up in them. Clearly the player cannot play his recovery from between a spectator's feet and so he retreats to a drop zone, an area that tries to replicate the situation he might have been left with had the stand not been there.

to how far back he can go; file disconsolately back to the spot from where he put himself in such a mess and have another bash.

Note: Several of the other rules, including those that govern forms of play, are dealt with in the next chapter, **Glossary**.

ETIQUETTE

Golf Rage

A new phrase entered the golfing vernacular in 1997 – Golf Rage. In truth there was nothing new about it at all: it had been around for years, albeit with no specific name. But inspired by Road Rage, Loud Music Rage and all the other things that drive normally sane people to irrational acts, Golf Rage was duly coined and made its way into the sporting consciousness.

Several instances of Golf Rage made headlines in the newspapers. There was the golfer who was so angered by a player who drove a ball into his group that he filed back in his direction, picked up the other man's club, and snapped it over his knee. In another example, two men started fighting in an argument over slow play, which ended with one taking the other to court for grievous bodily harm.

It is often said that golf brings out the best in people but, as these examples demonstrate, it can also bring out the worst. Almost invariably, the worst occurs because of the frustration felt when others are not versed in the wonderful art of etiquette – the code of manners that needs to be observed if golf is to be at all pleasurable. A full knowledge of the rules may be optional, but a full knowledge of the etiquette of golf is absolutely essential. For a start, not observing it can make the game a dangerous endeavour. A golf club, for example, is a lethal weapon in the hands of someone unaware of what the cry of 'Fore!' is all about.

Given its importance, then, it often amazes me how many golf books never mention etiquette within their pages. No wonder slow play has become such a problem on golf courses. No wonder we find an increasing amount of footprints in bunkers, and pitchmarks on greens. No wonder we have Golf Rage.

There are some peculiar traits about golf that come under the subject of etiquette that you will be familiar with even after a cursory following of the game on television. One only has to be within earshot of Nick Faldo's caddy Fanny Sunesson for thirty seconds, for example, to know that you have to stand still while her man is playing a shot. Another of her commands is to keep quiet. A third requests no cameras.

The reasons, you might ask? Because once a player has mastered the basic technique, a golf shot is primarily about the art of concentration and absolute concentration is not possible if a camera clicks, people are moving, or there is a tunnel of noise.

Basic Etiquette: an Imaginary Hole

Perhaps the easiest way to demonstrate some of the essentials of etiquette is to play an imaginary hole. So Faldo and Lee Westwood are standing on the tee. Faldo drives off first, having played the previous hole in the least number of strokes.

Westwood is on the right-hand side of the teeing

The importance of caddies: Depends completely upon the player. To some, his caddie is his best friend, his mentor, his psychologist and the man who tells him the yardage, the wind strength and reads the borrows on the greens. Oh, and he carries the bag as well. For other players, the caddie is useful for just the last of these tasks. For the best players, the caddie is ranked somewhere in between. It is not a coincidence, for example, that nearly all the top golfers have caddies who have been with them for a number of years. Once a bond of trust has been established, a caddie can certainly help with club judgement, and learn instinctively when a player needs encouragement. But the importance of a caddie can be overstated. At the end of the day, there's only one man who can play the shot, and it ain't the man carrying the bag.

Greg Norman tees off, with his fellow players out of his line of vision

area with the caddies, and all are facing Faldo. This is a basic courtesy to the man playing the shot. The last thing any player wants to see out of the corner of his eye while trying to play a shot is a playing partner shuffling or moving around behind him.

In an amateur game, if one of the group is left-handed, this can mean quite a bit of shuffling about on the tee, rather like cricketers swapping over fielding positions when a left-handed batsman comes to the crease.

Normally this provokes some comments along the lines of 'bloody left-handers,' or 'why can't you stand on the right side of the ball?' These comments always seem to produce a chuckle, but I invariably greet them with a malevolent stare. Maybe my left-handedness has something to do with it.

When playing his iron shot from the fairway Westwood takes a divot, which bounds on a few yards. While he is admiring his spiralling missile, his caddie is running on for the divot, carefully replacing it and treading softly over it before leaving the scene. There's nothing worse for a professional than to hit what appeared a perfect shot only to find it has finished in a divot.

Westwood's iron shot is every bit as good as it appeared from a distance and it has left its imprint in the green. He repairs it with the small implement specially made for the task.

Faldo, meanwhile, has missed the green wildly and the ball is heading for the spectators. Both he and Fanny yell 'Fore!' at the top of their voices. The spectators know this is the signal that the ball might be coming their way and cover their heads.

When on the green, both players take care to mind how they walk. Clearly, spike marks are an unavoidable curse of the profession but neither player wants to worsen the situation by impersonating an elephant. So many problems are caused to the surfaces of greens by spikes that a lot of clubs have now banned them altogether, ordering their members and visitors to wear shoes with spikeless soles. Will the tours follow this example and ban them from their events as well? There is a possibility.

Personally I'm in favour of retaining golf shoes with spikes in them, because there are other parts of the course, such as from a hilly lie, where a firm grip is essential if the shot is to be played properly. A firm grip is not possible in spikeless shoes.

One thing you will never see top players do but amateurs do all the time is lean on their putters while waiting to putt. This can leave indentations that all greens can do without.

Amateurs in pro tournaments: The easiest way for an amateur to get into a professional tournament is through a sponsor's invite. These will often be granted to someone who has won the British or US Amateur Championship. They're a way of expressing support for a player's achievements to date, and helping his progress. At the Open or US Open Championships, an amateur can earn his right to a place in the tournament by progressing from the pre-qualifying events. At the Masters, invitations are given, not earned.

Faldo's recovery from the crowd leaves him with a long putt and Sunesson asks him whether he would like the flag attended or out. He wants it attended and she holds it until the putt is on its way and then removes it long before the ball comes close to the hole (it is a two-shot penalty if a ball on the green comes into contact with a flagstick). Westwood wants the flag removed and his caddy sets it down by the side of the green, well out of harm's way.

Westwood's caddy takes care not to damage the edges of the hole when removing the flag. The holes are easy to deface and once that happens the edges curl in, and a four and a quarter inch hole loses some of its diameter. As every golfer quickly finds out, it is hard enough to get the ball to disappear when the hole is at its proper circumference, never mind smaller.

By now your head is probably spinning. How in heaven's name does any golfer remember all this? However, like driving a car or riding a bike, what appears impossible soon slots into place. Road Rage, I fear, will always be part of our lives. But at least with education Golf Rage should diminish.

Slow Play

Like the poor, slow play seems always to have been with us. Why would players have stopped driving from the green of the hole they had just finished and moved instead to a teeing ground designed for the purpose if not to speed up the game? Maybe it worked all those years ago. But it did not stop slow play. It has now infected all areas of the game to the extent that professionals think they are playing quickly if they complete a round in under four hours. Nothing promotes Golf Rage like slow play. I remember Colin Montgomerie's face as he walked off the 18th green after a five and half hour round at Loch Lomond a couple of years ago. Now granted, Monty is not the most placid of souls when he comes off the course, unless he has just gone round in something like 60. But this was something different altogether.

Nine times out of ten, Montgomerie is all sweetness and light if he is allowed fifteen minutes to work the madness out of his system. But an hour afterwards he was still ranting and I had every sympathy for him. I simply do not know how you can keep your concentration for five and a half hours.

The problem for amateur golfers is that the professionals are the role models and people who take up the game copy their mannerisms. The problem for viewers is that it makes for boring television. On both sides of the Atlantic both tours are taking steps to tackle slow play. At first this involved warning some of the journeymen without tackling the star culprits like Bernhard Langer and Nick Faldo. Tour officials have now stopped this obvious favouritism and watching golf has improved as a result. It is to be hoped they keep up the pressure.

To be fair, the professionals have the perfect excuse to be slow. When one shot can often mean the difference between tens of thousands of pounds, a few extra seconds is understandable. As of 1998, the European Tour is trying to speed things along by fining players £500 for a first offence and imposing a one-shot penalty for a second offence. This does seem to be working.

But what about amateurs? What is their excuse? No one will ever convince me that they enjoy the game any more for playing slowly. In fact I would wager my car on the fact they enjoy it less. I would wager my mortgage on the fact they make it less enjoyable for everyone else.

How to keep the traffic moving in professional events? It's easy really. The players should be ready to play when it is their turn and not start to assess the wind, the distance, and the club only when someone else has played; mark their cards while someone else is playing his shot; if practicable assess their putt while their playing partner is already trying to hole out.

Put so starkly, that previous paragraph might sound like I am trying to turn the pros into versions of Carl Lewis. But in reality golf is by its very nature a slow game, and why it is so important that people make a stand against slow play is because when it becomes too slow it turns a sport that is as appealing as any into the most boring game in the world.

That is why Colin Montgomerie ranted on that day at Loch Lomond, despite being surrounded by some of the most gorgeous scenery imaginable, and why he was right to do so.

Nick Faldo waits his turn on the 14th tee at Wentworth

A typical golf hole

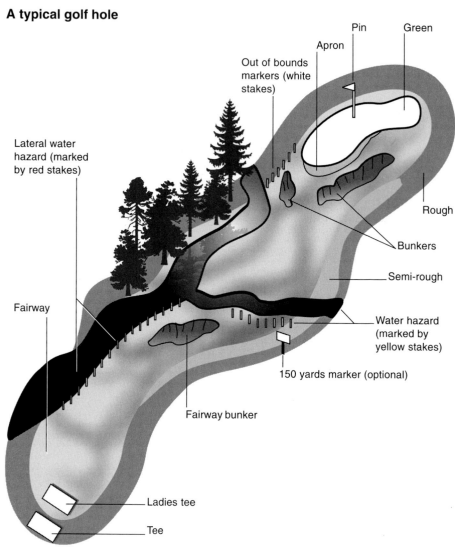

Pin
Green
Apron
Out of bounds
markers (white
stakes)
Lateral water
hazard (marked
by red stakes)
Rough
Bunkers
Semi-rough
Fairway
Water hazard
(marked by
yellow stakes)
150 yards marker (optional)
Fairway bunker
Ladies tee
Tee

Length and par: There is no set yardage
to determine the par for a hole.
However, normally a Par 3 hole is less
than 250 yards, and usually significantly
shorter. A Par 4 reaches its maximum at
480 yards, and longer than this is Par 5.
There is no Par 6.

Perhaps no sport, not even cricket or baseball, has developed such a comprehensive language of its own as golf. Imagine, for example, a passer-by tuning in to the following conversation: 'Three and two, that's right. Par, eagle, albatross. Holed a metal wood for that last one. His opponent had had a birdie too when he chipped stone dead from a tight lie. Canned his previous putt as well. A shame, really. He was very unlucky not to tee it up at the 17th.'

To a golfer, of course, it all makes perfect sense. To an outsider the dialogue might as well have taken place in some foreign tongue. 'Stone dead ... a shame, really' – was there a funeral or something?

Golf's rich language often alienates the outsider, who is intimidated by all the phrases and sayings. Here, then, is a glossary of the golfing dictionary, the unfathomable phrases, the leading competitions and venues, and those banal cliches that television commentators so bafflingly sometimes pluck out of the air.

A–Z of Golfing Terms

Even the most common words can mean something that is far from the obvious. For example ...

Ace
It is not: The number one guy, the leader of the pack.
It is: Nirvana – to have played a hole in one shot.

Address
It is not: The blurb you stick on an envelope.
It is: The position you adopt just before you play a shot.

Albatross

It is not: A millstone around your neck.
It is: Even better than an ace, actually – a score of three under par on a par four or par five.

Air shot

It is not: A ball played from a mountain.
It is: When you make an ass of yourself and completely miss the ball.

Apron

It is not: A frilly thing worn in the kitchen.
It is: The area at the front of a green.

Backspin

It is not: Backward rotation of a player celebrating a holed putt.
It is: Backward rotation of the ball in flight.

Backswing

It is not: An insult hurled while someone is looking the other way.
It is: The movement of the swing from the point of addressing the ball to the start of the downswing.

Balata

It is not: The sound of the ball when it hits the green.
It is: A substance for making the cover on certain types of golf balls.

Bent

It is not: A kink.
It is: A type of grass used on many American greens.

Better ball

It is not: A superior type of product.
It is: The best score of two players in a fourball competition.

Birdie

It is not: A flapping winged creature with two legs.
It is: A score of one under par on a hole. The term derives from an old American slang expression, 'what a bird', meaning something wonderful.

Blade

It is not: Something to keep in the bag in case things get unpleasant.
It is: The striking part of an iron club.

Blind shot

It is not: Undertaking a stroke with closed eyes.
It is: A shot where the target, or the fairway from the tee, is hidden from view.

Bogey

It is not: Something revolting hanging from an opponent's nose.
It is: A score of one over par on a hole. It derives from the old music hall saying: 'Hush, hush, here comes the bogey man, he will catch you if he can.'

Bogey competition

It is not: A tournament to be dreaded.
It is: A form of scoring in which competitors play against the par of the course, under matchplay rules.

Borrow

It is not: Asking your partner to lend you a tee.
It is: The natural slope in a green.

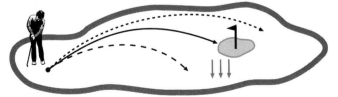

On target ——
'Overborrow' - - - - -
'Underborrow' – – –

Break

It is not: Coffee and biscuits at the halfway house.
It is: The same as borrow.

Bunker

It is not: A golfer with a stubborn mentality.
It is: A sandpit, defined as a hazard, into which one's ball flies all too often.

Caddy or caddie

It is not: A tea-holder.
It is: A person employed to carry a golf bag.

Caddie cart

It is not: Transport for the benefit of a caddie.
It is: Transport that does the job of a caddie

Carry

It is not: The art of lugging a bag around a course.
It is: The distance over a hazard.

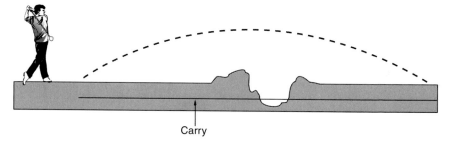

Carry

Cack-handed

It is not: Someone with dirty hands.
It is: A derogatory term for a left-handed golfer.

Casual water

It is not: Water with attitude.
It is: Standing water on a course that is not part of a hazard.

Charge
It is not: An electrifying surge by a player.
It is: A recklessly bold putt.

Chip
It is not: A sulking golfer.
It is: A short approach shot, played low with little backspin.

Choke
It is not: Someone struggling for breath on a golf course.
It is: Someone struggling for breath on a golf course. Well sort of. It means throwing away a tournament when in position to win.

Closed stance
It is not: Someone not prepared to change their point of view.
It is: The position adopted at address when a player wants to draw or hook the ball.

Compression
It is not: A golfer with the weight of the world on his shoulders.
It is: The degree of resilience of a golf ball.

Cut
It is not: A nasty wound suffered during a round.
It is: A shot that has veered off horribly to the right. And the mark in a tournament, usually after 36 holes, whereby the field is divided into those who play on and those who go home.

Dead
It is not: Someone who has been badly hit by a golf ball.
It is: A ball so close to the hole it is unmissable.

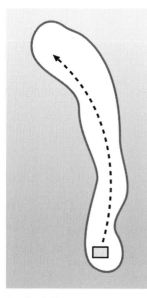

Dogleg left

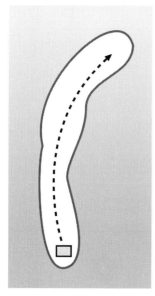

Dogleg right

Dogleg

It is not: A club shaft that has collided with a tree.
It is: A hole with a fairway that turns sharply to the left or right.

Dormie

It is not: Lodgings in the clubhouse.
It is: In matchplay, standing as many holes up as there are holes remaining to be played.

Double bogey

It is not: Something revolting hanging from a nostril.
It is: A score of two over par on one hole.

Draw

It is not: An invitation for pretty pictures on your scorecard.
It is: A shot that curves moderately to the left.

Drive

It is not: Anything to do with motoring.
It is: A shot from the tee.

Driving range

It is not: Somewhere to do handbreak turns.
It is: Somewhere to practise your golf.

Duck-hook

It is not: Something to fish your ball out of water.
It is: A drive that curves sharply to the left.

Eagle

It is not: A high, soaring shot.
It is: A score of two under par on a hole.

Explosion shot

It is not: A stroke that leaves you raging.
It is: A bunker shot

Fade
It is not: Someone falling from contention.
It is: Controlled shot that curves gently to the right.

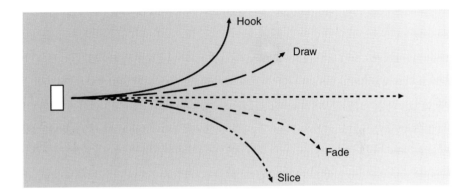

Fairway
It is not: A shot that has a long distance to travel.
It is: The mown area of grass you are trying to hit with your drive.

Fat
It is not: Anything to do with obesity.
It is: A shot where the ground is hit before the ball.

Fluff
It is not: Those nice furry headcovers that are the rage these days.
It is: A mishit shot. And the nickname of Tiger Woods's caddie.

Follow through
It is not: Letting someone pass if you are slow.
It is: The motion of the swing from impact onwards.

Fore!
It is not: A polite variation on a well-known four-letter word.

It is: The shouted warning to other players that a ball is heading in their direction.

Gimme

It is not: Someone being cheeky.
It is: A conceded putt in matchplay.

Grain

It is not: Australian for green.
It is: The direction in which the blades of grass on a putting green predominantly lie.

Gross

It is not: A disgusting shot.
It is: The score actually made before deduction of handicap.

Handicap

It is not: Anything to do with disability or weights.
It is: A compensation in shots applied to enable golfers to compete on approximately level terms.

Heel

It is not: A term for a golfer of disreputable character.
It is: The near end of a clubhead at address.

Hickory

It is not: An invitation to start singing nursery rhymes.
It is: The wood from which shafts were made before steel and graphite and other materials came into use.

Home

It is not: A reference to where you live.
It is: The last nine holes of an eighteen-hole golf course.

Handicap: This is allocated by the handicap committee of a golf club and is initially calculated on the average of the member's first three score cards submitted in competition. Cards then have to be regularly handed in to maintain handicap. The highest male handicap is 28, the lowest is scratch, ie 0. All touring professionals play off scratch.

Honour

It is not: A gong for winning the monthly medal.
It is: The privilege of playing first from the tee.

Hook

It is not: Anything to do with Henry Cooper, keen golfer though he is.
It is: A golf shot that curves out of control to the left.

Interlocking

It is not: A husband and wife golf pairing.
It is: A grip whereby the little finger of the right hand interlocks with the forefinger of the left hand.

Overlapping grip

Lag

It is not: An old golfer who has been around a while.
It is: A putt played to get close to but short of the hole.

Lie

It is not: Anything to do with fibbing.
It is: Where the ball has come to rest.

Links

It is not: Golf courses in Lincolnshire.
It is: The land upon which seaside golf courses are built.

Interlocking grip

Local rules

It is not: Some sly regulations introduced by the home player in order to give him a better chance of winning.
It is: Regulations that apply to a particular course. In Florida, for example, you might see a local rule that allows you to pick and drop away from a sunbathing alligator, without penalty.

Strong grip
This is when three or more knuckles of the left hand are visible at address and tends to lead to a hook.

Weak grip
One or less knuckles are visible and tends to a slice.

Loft
It is not: Anything to do with the clubhouse attic.
It is: The angle in degrees of a club face.

Loose impediments
It is not: Unruly children.
It is: Unattached natural objects that might affect a shot.

Matchplay
It is not: Making models from matches.
It is: A competition which is decided by the number of holes won.

Medal competition
It is not: An award ceremony where they hand out all the honours.
It is: A strokeplay tournament, usually held once a month at most clubs.

Mulligan
It is not: A drop of the hard stuff on the first tee.
It is: A second chance should you fail to do your stuff on the first tee.

Open stance
It is not: Someone who can't make up their mind.
It is: The position adopted at address when someone wants to deliberately push or slice the ball.

Out of bounds
It is not: The captain's wife.
It is: Everywhere that lies outside the areas defined as the course.

Outside agency
It is not: A form of industrial tribunal.
It is: Any object, including a person who is not

part of the game, that stops, deflects or moves a ball in play.

Overlapping grip

It is not: A man taking on more than he can handle.
It is: A method of holding the club whereby the little finger of the right hand overlaps the space between the forefinger and second finger of the left hand.

Pairing

It is not: The happy union of two golfers.
It is: Two players drawn together in strokeplay competition.

Par

It is not: A friendly reference to a senior golfer.
It is: The standard score in strokes assigned to a hole, and to a round, of a given course.

Pin

It is not: Anything to do with sharp needles.
It is: The flagstick.

Pin high

It is not: How tall your opponent is.
It is: An approach that has travelled approximately the distance that separated you from the flag.

Pitch

It is not: The level of noise expected when shouting 'Fore!'
It is: A short approach shot, invariably over a bunker or rough terrain, with a steep trajectory and (hopefully) considerable backspin.

Pitch mark

It is not: Graffiti on the grass.

Normal grip
Two knuckles visible. Should be straight, everything else considered.
However, many top professionals have pronounced strong or weak grips and manage very nicely. Practice is all.

It is: Indent left by a ball when it lands on the green.

Pivot
It is not: A mild form of rebuke for a bad shot.
It is: Rotation of the body during a golf swing.

Pot bunker
It is not: A sand trap where you can smoke illegal substances.
It is: A deep, usually small bunker with steep sides.

Preferred lies
It is not: Superior tall tales told in the clubhouse.
It is: The ability to be able to drop and clean your ball during the winter or following unusually inclement weather.

Provisional
It is not: A golf game subject to cancellation.
It is: A reserve ball played to save time when it seems possible the first one is lost or out of bounds.

Pull
It is not: A successful liaison in the mixed foursomes.
It is: A ball that flies off in a straight line to the left.

Push
It is not: An unsuccessful liaison in the mixed foursomes.
It is: A ball that flies off in a straight line to the right.

Rabbit
It is not: Anything to do with Watership Down.
It is: A golfer of minuscule ability.

Rough
It is not: A golfer who looks like he has been up all

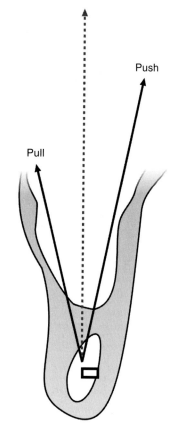

Push

Pull

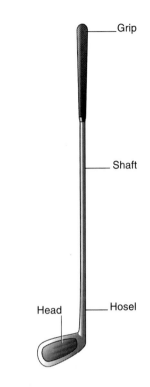

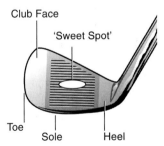

Grip

Shaft

Head

Hosel

Club Face

'Sweet Spot'

Toe

Sole

Heel

the night before.

It is: The areas of grass lining each side of the fairway that have been allowed to grow.

Royal and Ancient

It is not: The Queen.

It is: The Royal and Ancient Golf Club of St Andrews, the game's governing body and overseer of the rules.

Scrambled

It is not: The state of your brain after a bad golfing day.

It is: The ability to rescue a good score despite not playing particularly well.

Scratch

It is not: Anything to do with skin that is irritated.

It is: A player who competes off a handicap of nought.

Set-up

It is not: A player who is duped.

It is: A player's address position.

Shank

It is not: A watery grave for your golf ball.

It is: To hit the ball with the hosel (see diagram) of an iron club.

Slice

It is not: Your share of the winnings.

It is: An uncontrolled shot where the ball veers sharply to the right.

Sole

It is not: Lunch.

It is: The bottom of a golf club.

The majority of amateurs use 'cavity-backed' clubs, which supposedly offer a more reliable 'sweet spot'. Professionals tend to favour cast-iron, solid backs – known as 'blades' – which provide the top golfer with more feel and control.

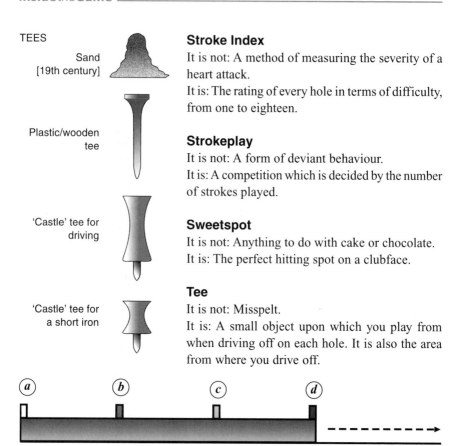

TEES

Sand
[19th century]

Plastic/wooden
tee

'Castle' tee for
driving

'Castle' tee for
a short iron

Stroke Index
It is not: A method of measuring the severity of a heart attack.
It is: The rating of every hole in terms of difficulty, from one to eighteen.

Strokeplay
It is not: A form of deviant behaviour.
It is: A competition which is decided by the number of strokes played.

Sweetspot
It is not: Anything to do with cake or chocolate.
It is: The perfect hitting spot on a clubface.

Tee
It is not: Misspelt.
It is: A small object upon which you play from when driving off on each hole. It is also the area from where you drive off.

The tee
a) Championship tee, used in major competitions
b) Medal tee, used in club competitions
c) Men's tee, used in friendly matches
d) Women's/juniors' tee, often separate from the main tee

Thin
It is not: A golfer who has been on a diet.
It is: A shot where the blade of the iron only catches the top half of the ball.

Tight
It is not: A derogatory name for Scottish golfers.
It is: A narrow fairway or entrance to the green.

Topped
It is not: A suicidal golfer.
It is: A shot that travels all along the ground.

Trap
It is not: A cunning plan to win a match.
It is: A bunker.

Turn
It is not: A golfer who suddenly falls ill.
It is: The halfway point in a match.

Vardon grip
It is not: Anything to do with the freemasons.
It is: The overlapping grip.

Yips
It is not: Some terrible disease that brings you out in spots.
It is: Some terrible disease affecting the nervous system that plays havoc with either your chipping or putting or both.

Golfing Phrases

Naturally, along with all the words, golf has developed its own phraseology. Indeed, watch any of the broadcasts from America, and they appear to come up with a new phrase every week, usually complete with tortured syntax. Here is a selection of the more common phrases that one might come across and what they're supposed to explain.

'He's chili-dipped that one.'

Quite how chili-dip, a Mexican hors d'oeuvre, came to mean mis-hitting a lofted approach shot to a green by striking the ground first, is anyone's guess. The most famous chili-dip in recent times came at St Andrews in 1995, and the victim was Costantino Rocca on the 18th hole of the final round. However, this was one occasion when the mistake was not costly – he made amends by holing the consequent 70ft putt to force a play-off.

'It has gone in on the fly.'

Another one from America – where else? – this means holing your approach shot without the ball having bounced on its way into the hole. One famous example of this came in the 1989 Open at Royal Troon, and Mark Calcavecchia's shot from the rough to the side of the 12th green. What appeared likely to be a six on his card instead became a three and he went on to win the event in a four-hole play-off.

'This surely calls for a chip and run shot.'

No, nothing to do with stretching the legs and trying to keep up with the ball. This simply means that a chip shot, when it hits the green, will not spin and instead roll towards the hole. At least that is what will happen if it is played correctly. A variation is the pitch and run shot.

Occasionally you will hear commentators talk about a 'bump and run' shot. This happens if the green has a steep bank to negotiate, and there are circumstances which negate a conventional pitch shot. So the player will bump it into the bank and hope to see it hop up and run across the green towards the hole.

'You certainly got the rub of the green there.'

This is a polite way of saying that a player has had a piece of good luck. In my fourball the same information is normally conveyed by the saying: 'You lucky (insert swear word of the day here).'

'If he's going to get up he is going to need a long iron.'

To get up means to reach the green. Long irons take their name from their slightly longer shafts and generally refer to any club from a one iron to a four iron. From five to seven are considered mid-irons, and eight upwards are short irons.

'Now, can he get up and down from there?'

Up and down refers to the art of getting the ball from a particular position and into the hole in two shots. It is an art too. Raymond Floyd was a master at getting up and down from 70 yards; Gary Player was brilliant at getting up and down from bunkers; and Phil Mickelson is the modern day wizard at getting up and down from trouble around a green.

'He needs to play smart here and take the hazard out of play.'

Well, it would be nice if the words could be taken literally wouldn't it? The lake is looking ominous so we just call in the bulldozers and ask for it to be removed. Now, surprise, surprise, it doesn't mean this at all. What the commentator means is the player should select a club which would mean he could not reach the hazard even if he hit his very best shot. That way it ceases to be a consideration and, hence, 'out of play'.

'Dropped a shot.'
All sorts of ideas must run through the mind of the golfing beginner when he hears this common phrase on television. It means, simply, that a player has failed by one stroke in his efforts to record a par on the hole he has just completed.

'Through the back door.'
This phrase makes absolutely no sense at all, yet has become part of the commentator's lingo. How can holes that are round have doors, even imaginary ones? Through the back door means a putt that appears to be slipping beyond the hole but which falls in at the last possible moment.

'Scampered away.'
Often heard when a tournament is being played on fast greens. Sometimes the hole will be situated on a mound and if a player has misjudged the speed he can look foolish, as the ball skips well past the hole without giving it a second glance: hence, it has scampered away.

What is in a Golf Bag?

The essential items are a set of clubs (up to fourteen, including a putter), a box of tees, at least six golf balls, a pencil and a pitchmark repairer. These days, a professional's bag will also include a pouch for his watch and jewellery, a box of plasters, a piece of fruit, Mars bars, granola bars, a jumper – heck, play is so slow these days there's probably an up-to-date index of his share prices he can look at to keep him happy between shots. If the weather is inclement a set of waterproofs and an umbrella are also vital, and some form of headgear if you like that sort of thing.

As for the clubs, there was a time when the pros roughly agreed on the fourteen implements that would find their way into the bag. There would be a driver and three wood: every iron from one to nine, plus a wedge and a sand wedge; and a putter. Now, anything goes. Some pros carry three woods and make do without a one or two iron. The players who are wonders around the greens will often take three wedges; John Daly often carries four wedges and makes do with just one wood.

With regard to amateurs, many older players have taken to carrying as many as five woods, as they find the long irons harder to strike well and prefer a wood with a greater loft. The accompanying table illustrates the specifications of many of the clubs that are available these days and how far an average pro and amateur should expect to hit them.

Type	Loft	Avge. Prof's dist.	Avge. Amateur's dist.
Driver	10 degrees	270 yds	235 yds
Three wood	15 degrees	245 yds	215 yds
Five wood	21 degrees	210 yds	190 yds
One iron	15 degrees	235 yds	Not applicable
Two iron	18 degrees	220 yds	195 yds
Three iron	22 degrees	200 yds	180 yds
Four iron	26 degrees	190 yds	170 yds
Five iron	30 degrees	180 yds	160 yds
Six iron	34 degrees	170 yds	150 yds
Seven iron	38 degrees	160 yds	140 yds
Eight iron	42 degrees	150 yds	130 yds
Nine iron	46 degrees	140 yds	120 yds
Wedge	50 degrees	130 yds	110 yds
Sand wedge	56 degrees	100 yds	70 yds

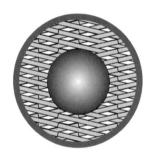

Golf Balls

As we have already seen, the choice available when buying a golf ball is immense and terribly confusing to anyone who is not well versed in what has happened in the industry over the last decade.

But they are all the same aren't they? This is the oft-heard cry and a quite understandable one when faced with such a bewildering selection. In fact, golf balls are far from all the same. A 24 handicapper, for example, who played the same ball as the professionals use, would find himself having to change ball every two or three holes because of the damage he would do to it.

So, here's a simplified guide. For the above player, the magic words on the packaging are 'two piece distance ball'. As the words imply, these balls supply a few more yards and will not easily cut or be scuffed and therefore should last for several rounds, always assuming they have not been despatched into a lake.

Why doesn't every golfer use this type of ball, you might ask. After all, doesn't everyone want to hit the ball further? Well, maybe, but the thing that goes with a distance ball is control with shots to and around the greens. Hit a chip with a distance ball and it won't stop rolling. For a 24 handicapper this does not matter, but for a player who has learned to strike the ball properly, there is nothing worse than seeing an iron shot struck well from distance and then watching it roll through the green. Most mid to low handicappers could make significant improvements simply by switching to a ball that imparts more spin.

The professionals are always experimenting with different golf balls, always presuming, of course, they are made by the manufacturers who are handing over big bucks to play their products.

Greg Norman went through a phase where he was imparting so much backspin on the ball that it was spinning off the front of greens. He was also concerned that he was giving too much yardage away off the tee to players like Tiger Woods.

So Norman has switched to a ball that flies with a slightly lower trajectory. This means it will roll further, giving him more distance, and spin less, because it is landing on greens with a slightly flatter plane.

Ten Golf Organisations Worth Committing to Memory

Professional Golfers' Association European Tour (PGAET)

The European Tour, which is based at Wentworth, looks after the interests of all tournament professionals in Europe. It began life in 1971 and

Wentworth

has enjoyed a remarkable existence, expanding rapidly during the halcyon years for European golf in the mid-1980s and maintaining a steady growth ever since. In 1976, the total prize money played for on the European Tour was £874,878. Twenty years later it came to in excess of £29 million.

Professional Golfers' Association (PGA)

The PGA was formed in 1901 to look after the interests of all British professionals. Now it concentrates primarily on the affairs of the club pros, although the Ryder Cup, which it runs jointly with the European Tour whenever the match is held in Europe, is still within its remit. Its headquarters are at the Belfry, near Birmingham.

The Belfry

Professional Golfers' Association Tour (PGA Tour)

Often referred to in Britain as the US Tour to avoid confusion with other similarly named bodies. The PGA Tour is the largest and most successful professional tour in the world. In 1998 it celebrated its sixtieth anniversary. Though the growth in the number of events has not been dramatic – thirty-eight then as opposed to forty-five now – the same cannot be said for prize money. In 1938 this totalled $158,000. Sixty years on it came to – a deep breath now – $94,080,000. The PGA Tour's headquarters are in Ponte Vedra, Florida.

Professional Golfers' Association of America (PGA of America)

Ostensibly they are the equivalent of the British PGA in that they handle the affairs of club professionals, but it is a body with much more glamour: for a start, they are solely responsible for the Ryder Cup whenever it is held in America. They also organise the USPGA Championship, which is one of the sport's four majors.

Ladies Professional Golfers' Association Tour (LPGA Tour)

Based at Daytona Beach, Florida, the women's equivalent of the PGA Tour is immensely successful in its own right with annual prize money in excess of $30 million. In the 1990s the tour has become spectacularly cosmopolitan with its four leading stars comprising one player from Britain (Laura Davies), one from Sweden (Annika Sorenstam), one from America (Kelly Robbins), and one from Australia (Karrie Webb).

Women Professional Golfers' European Tour (WPGET)

The Women's European Tour has been the great puzzlement of professional golf in recent years. On the one hand its members have enjoyed spectacular successes. On the other the more they achieve the less tournaments they seem to have to play in each year. By 1998 the situation had deteriorated to the extent that just seven published events were sure to take place at the start of the season. It was a far cry from ten years earlier when there were over twenty. The WPGET began life in 1979 and is based at Tytherington Golf Club, Macclesfield.

Royal and Ancient Golf Club of St Andrews (R&A)

For 101 years the R&A have been the game's governing body for everywhere outside the United States. They make the rules and apply decisions to those rules. They also run the Open and the Amateur Championship, among other events.

St Andrews

Membership of the Royal and Ancient is limited to 1,800, of whom 1,800 are men. According to Michael Bonallack, the R&A's secretary, 'this is not a question of chauvinism'. Of course not. Perish the thought, old boy.

United States Golf Association (USGA)

Based in New Jersey, the USGA is America's national governing body. It runs United States Opens for both men and women – the former one of the four major championships, the latter the greatest prize in the women's game – and the US Amateur Championship. Alongside the R&A, the USGA has the power to change the rules and how the game is played. Currently they are undertaking exhaustive studies into the effects on the game of new technology.

Home Golf Unions

In all there are four in the UK – the English, Scottish, Welsh, and Irish Golf Unions. They administer the amateur side of the game at grass roots level and host a number of competitions for the leading practitioners. Many of these players have gone on to become top professionals, including Nick Faldo, and Sandy Lyle. The English Golf Union (EGU) is the biggest of the four and in 1995 moved into purpose-built premises at one on the country's leading courses, Woodhall Spa, in Lincolnshire.

Ladies Golf Union (LGU)

Administers the women's amateur game in Britain from its headquarters in St Andrews. Formed in 1893, it organises the British Amateur Championship and the Curtis Cup, among other events, and regulates the handicapping system for women.

Ten Essential Tournaments
to Watch on Television

OPEN VENUES

St Andrews
Muirfield
Lytham St Annes
Birkdale
Royal St George's
Turnberry
Troon
Carnoustie

1. The Open Championship (July)

The game's oldest and most glittering prize, the tournament rotates between eight links courses situated in England and Scotland. Sadly, the demands of the modern championship, with spectator facilities for 40,000 people a day, hospitality villages and exhibition tents, mean that this number will never be lifted. The R&A have never contemplated holding the event anywhere but a seaside course and they should not either. It adds a unique element to what is already one of the world's great sporting events.

2. The Masters (April)

Sometimes called the US Masters in Britain but, rather as the Open needs merely the definite article to distinguish it, so the Masters. It is always held in the second week in April at a course in Georgia called Augusta National. The first of golf's four major championships every year, it is also the youngest, having begun life in 1934. A year later Gene Sarazen holed a wooden shot from the fairway at the 15th for an albatross to set up an unlikely victory. It also set the pattern for much that has gone on since: the Masters is frequently the most exciting of the four grand slam events.

3. United States Open (June)

The strangest of golf's four majors since it has a list of winners that include all the great names in the sport's history and some decidedly obscure ones as well. Like Andy North, for instance. He only won three events in his professional career and yet two of them were US Opens. So the record books state he won as many majors as Greg Norman and yet any other comparison between the two players does not bare the remotest scrutiny. The event is taken around the United States with no set rota. In 1999 it will visit new territory when it is hosted by Pinehurst in North Carolina.

4. PGA Championship (August)

All of golf's four majors have a subtitle and the PGA's is that it is the weakest. Part of the problem is that it comes too soon after the Open. It would be much better if it was pushed back into late September but by then the US television networks are into their football coverage and, well, we cannot disturb that, can we? Began life as a matchplay event which some people would like to see it revert to, to give it a bit more character. The PGA of America, however, are happy with the present format. The event has been given a lift in recent years by visiting some of the great American venues, like Winged Foot, New York, in 1997.

5. Ryder Cup
(Every odd-number year, September)

In all of sport there cannot be a more dramatic rise to prominence than that achieved by this biennial tournament. Just fifteen years ago it was a backwater event as the Americans yawned their way to another victory over first, Great Britain and Ireland, and then Europe when the rules were adapted. Now that European golf has improved out of all recognition, it is a different story, with the tournament's classic design, with three different formats over the three days, seen to brilliant effect. Since 1983 the

Europeans have won four matches, the Americans three, with one tied. In those eight contests, only one has been decided by a margin of two points or more in either team's favour. The result has been an event that has transcended golf to become sporting theatre of the most dramatic kind.

6. The Players' Championship (March)

I'm with those who hope there will never be a fifth major in golf but this, unquestionably, is the best event to win outside the four tournaments that comprise the grand slam. Held each year at the PGA Tour's headquarters in Florida, it always boasts the strongest field. This is another tournament that would probably benefit from a change of date, since at present it is staged just two weeks before the Masters. Accordingly, it is seen by many players as a dress rehearsal for Augusta. It actually deserves much more respect than that.

7. The United States Women's Open (July)

Although most male golfers consider the Open the most prized of the four majors, it is not a unanimous verdict. Some prefer the Masters; a lot of Americans would vote for their national Open. On the distaff side of the game, there is no argument. This event is head and shoulders above the rest and its list of winners reflects the fact.

8. The Solheim Cup (September)

For a tournament that only began life in 1990, the Solheim Cup has quickly come of age. The women's equivalent of the Ryder Cup, the Americans are currently leading the series 3–1 and the nature of their comfortable triumph in 1996 at St Pierre has led to worries in some quarters that it may become a drone, with non-stop, easy victories for the US. St Pierre proved one indisputable fact: matchplay golf makes for pulsating viewing when the games are close, but when they are one-sided the fare is dull, dull, dull. Still, let us not be too pessimistic. The tour might have collapsed around their ears but there is surely no reason why the Europeans cannot field a team of twelve players every other year and make a match of it.

9. Volvo PGA Championship (May)

The flagship event of the European Tour, it is staged every May at Wentworth. The West Course has all the ingredients that go towards making a fine, exciting venue. The last two holes are both par fives, both reachable in two but the 17th in particular is more likely to yield a seven than a three. In the Autumn the West course dons a different face for the World Matchplay event, when it is dressed in dazzling greens and golds. The trouble is the tournament these days has only half the excitement it possessed in its early days when it lived up to its grandiose title.

10. World Championship of Golf – Matchplay (February)

A curious choice one may think, given that the event has not actually taken place yet. This new tournament, to be staged at La Costa, California, in February 1999, will be the first of the four World Championship of Golf events demanded by the players who want to see more of each other in competition. It promises to be the most exciting of the four since the format will be matchplay and the top sixty-four players on the World Ranking will be the competitors. A curious choice, as I say, but I for one can hardly wait.

TEN OTHER RECOMMENDED TOURNAMENTS

1. Doral Open (PGA Tour, March)
2. Bay Hill Invitational (PGA Tour, March)
3. Benson and Hedges International (European Tour, May)
4. Western Open (PGA Tour, July)
5. Irish Open (European Tour, July)
6. Loch Lomond Invitational (European Tour, July)
7. World Series of Golf (PGA Tour, August)
8. The Tour Championship (PGA Tour, October/ November)
9. World Championship of Golf: Strokeplay (Europe, Nov.)
10. Australian Open (Australian Tour, December)

Ten Courses that Look Wonderful on Television

1. Old Course, St Andrews

The links of St Andrews

Summary: 500 years old and still it looks great in front of the cameras. The Alfred Dunhill Cup

is a terribly contrived golf tournament and
normally I wouldn't recommend it unless it was
opposite the wrestling. But it is staged annually at
St Andrews and you would have to be made of stone
not to be moved as the camera pans around to reveal
some of the finest architecture in Scotland. The golf
course is not bad either. The Dunhill Cup is held at
a time of year when the town is at its finest. This is
October, when the tourists have moved out and the
students are back. Then, once more, St Andrews is
slave not to one but both of the things – golf and
learning – that have rightly made it famous.

Key hole and how to play it: The 17th hole is
deservedly the most fabled on the course. It is a long
par four that thrives on torturing its victims. If the out
of bounds to the right off the tee does not get a player
there is always the notorious bunker that eats into the
front of the green. In the 1995 Open Costantino Rocca
needed three shots to extract himself from it in his
play-off against John Daly. Then there is the road to
worry about behind the shallow green.

The ideal tee shot bravely bites off much of the
corner of the grounds of the Old Course Hotel,
leaving a player with a long iron to the green. Most
players then play for the right of the bunker, hoping
to leave the ball pin-high, some 35ft away, and
then two putt for par. The fun at the Dunhill Cup,
which has a hybrid matchplay format, comes if a
player needs a birdie to try to catch his opponent
and so has to gamble with the hazards.

2. Pebble Beach, Monterey, California

Summary: Robert Louis Stevenson called the
Monterey Peninsula the greatest meeting of land
and sea in the world: then they went and improved

it by building the greatest stretch of ocean holes known to man. Pebble Beach is seen on satellite television every January when the AT&T pro-am comes to town. In 2000 it will host the US Open. From the 109-yard 7th hole to the raw power of the daunting two par fours that follow, this is golf at its finest. But it is the 17th and 18th that will have you on the edge of your seat, the last running right along the edge of the cliff-top. Lose a ball here and the nearest piece of land not nearer the hole is Hawaii.

The 7th hole at Pebble Beach

Key hole: The 17th should be a pivotal hole on every golf course and Pebble Beach suitably meets the criteria. It is a long par three played towards the Pacific and frequently into the prevailing wind. There is no great strategy required to play it; the only prerequisite is to find the putting surface. This is no easy matter on a calm day, never mind when the Californian elements are at their worst. In the

1982 US Open Jack Nicklaus was quite happy to sit in the clubhouse knowing that Tom Watson would need to par both the 17th and 18th to force a play-off. He was even happier when Watson hooked his tee shot at the former into thick rough. What followed next was one of the great shots, as Watson chipped in for a birdie. Yet the perils of missing the green were still well illustrated. If Watson's chip had not hit the flag dead centre then the green's natural slopes would have taken the ball 20ft away. On such flimsy margins can the fate of major championships be decided.

3. Augusta National, Georgia

Summary: Watching the Masters on television each April has inspired so many golfers to take up the game it is almost a cliche. Lee Westwood was one, after watching Nicklaus in 1986; Nick Faldo was another, after watching Nicklaus in 1971.

Augusta National

Augusta is impossible to play without an invite to the Masters or an invite from one of its select group of 300 members. So, naturally, it tops every list as the course that everyone wants to play. Each April it is at its finest; the Georgia spring is in full bloom, the dogwoods and rhododendrons are everywhere, the fairways are like bowling greens, and the putting surfaces glisten like polished crystal. The result is a course of unimaginable beauty that is perfectly playable for the most humble of amateurs but which still trips up the most talented of professionals. What a feat of ingenuity.

Key hole: Such is the spectacular nature of Augusta's inward nine that every hole is a key hole. The stretch known as Amen Corner – the 11th, 12th, and 13th holes – have probably decided more Masters titles than any other, and of these the par three 12th can be a killer. Known as the Golden Bell, it has tolled for too many to count. At 155 yards it does not sound menacing and from the tee the green looks inviting enough. Trouble is: the putting surface is a mere sliver; Rae's Creek, complete with steep bank, catches any shot that comes up short, as does a perilous bunker; further sand traps catch any shot long; and then there is the tee itself, sheltered from the wind and so making club selection hazardous. Television producers know their trade. These days, after a player has hit his shot to the 12th, the camera will stay on his face. Watch for the almost palpable sense of relief when the ball plunges down on to the green.

4. Emirates Course, Dubai

Summary: This venue is testament to the wonders of modern technology and what it has done for golf course architecture. To take 300 acres of flat, arid desert, 20 minutes from the centre of Dubai, and turn it into a hilly, immaculately green course filled with superbly challenging holes leaves one breathless in admiration. The course is sprayed with one million gallons of water daily to keep it green. Each February it plays host to the Dubai Desert Classic and it speaks volumes for the course that the event is frequently among the most exciting each year on the European Tour.

Key hole: The 18th is a par five that dog-legs to the left, with water in front of the green. The drive is frequently played into the wind but the green is usually in reach with a long iron or wooden club. The fun begins if a competitor needs to birdie it, say, to make a play-off. Then we see if he is on his mettle. In 1996 Colin Montgomerie was certainly on his mettle, hitting his metal driver from the tee and then again from the fairway to set up his winning birdie. The latter was declared the shot of the year.

5. Valderrama, Andalucia, Spain

Summary: Not even the worst storms to be seen on the Costa del Sol for more than ten years could ruin Valderrama as a spectacle. The course still looked in fantastic condition for the 1997 Ryder Cup, which had something to do with the fact that it was. The vast amounts spent on proper drainage were truly rewarded. A normal course of this quality would have 600 sprinkler heads to keep it properly watered; Valderrama has 4,600. Nor is the water in the hazards dyed blue, as is sometimes the case at Augusta. 'It would kill off our otters', Valderrama's owner, Jaime Patino, explains. Valderrama will return to television screens in November, 1999 when it hosts the World Championship of Golf strokeplay tournament.

Key hole: The Americans hated it; Colin Montgomerie thinks it the worst hole in European golf. What cannot be disputed is that the 17th makes for undeniably enthralling television. The cause of the professionals' ire is a band of rough that runs across the fairway at the 280-yard mark, thereby limiting the length of the drive. Now a tricky decision has to be made. Does one go for a green which is protected to the front by water and to the rear by bunkers? Or does one lay up short? The hole was redesigned by Severiano Ballesteros and one of the things I like is the fact that even if a player lays up short, the pitch is a tricky one, since the green tilts severely back towards the water. The onus, then, is to have a bash in two.

6. West Course, Wentworth

Summary: The World Matchplay Championship has been held at Wentworth every year since 1964. In the early years it was the tournament that made the headlines; these days, as the event's prestige has slipped, it is the course that draws most of the plaudits. And quite right too. In a dry spring or summer it can get a touch bouncy but by the autumn it invariably plays as it was meant to be played: long and daunting, but never less than picturesque. As previously mentioned, the West Course also plays host each May to the Volvo PGA Championship, but it is as a matchplay venue – it also hosted the 1953 Ryder Cup – that it has become rightly acclaimed.

Key hole: The 17th once more, a wonderful par five that winds and twists for much of its 570 yards. The drive is a perilous one, with out of bounds to the left and trees and deep rough to the right. The fairway tilts sharply to the right and so the ideal drive is one that flirts with the out of bounds before taking the natural contours on first bounce. Now the green is within reach but still a shot of immense skill is required to find it. The out of bounds continues to be a problem down the left, so thwarting the player seeking to draw the ball to gain a few more yards. The 17th can see any score from three to ten. Which makes it a wonderful hole in any language, and most certainly television's.

Wentworth

7. Turnberry, Ayrshire

Summary: The eight venues on the Open Championship rota all have their relative merits. People talk about the dunes when they mention Birkdale, the tradition of St Andrews, the fairness of Muirfield, and the terrifying difficulty of Carnoustie. At Turnberry it is the beauty of its stretch of seaside holes and on television, with the ornamental lighthouse standing guard over the 9th hole, they look spectacular. On top of the hill, way behind the 18th green, stands the equally stunning Turnberry hotel, restored to its full lustre and now as good as any in Britain.

Key hole: The 10th perhaps comes too early to be considered truly the key hole but it is certainly one to watch for on television. It completes the stretch of seaside holes and is perhaps the best in terms of quality. The hole winds its way around the craggy shore, past the remains of a castle, the site of some of Robert the Bruce's stirring deeds. On the right is a war monument that commemorates those who died in the First World War. The fairway is broad but the second shot is a difficult one to an amply protected green. Dinna Fouter is the name of the hole and it is hard not to fouter if the wind is coming in off the sea.

8. Crans-sur-Sierre, Switzerland

With regard to television, it certainly helps when a course is perched 5,000ft up a Swiss mountain with dazzling views from every hole. Every September the course plays host to the European Masters and while some of the holes are exceedingly average and the greens in 1997 were a disgrace, most of the players took the view that it was still a pretty splendid place to be. Crans, resort to the rich and famous, is also the only week of the year where the golfers on the European Tour get to feel like relative paupers.

Key hole: Look out for the 7th, for the view from behind the tee is one of the most breathtaking in golf. The hole measures just over 302 yards and the green is frequently driven. It is one of the easiest holes but sometimes such holes can exert the most pressure. Every player who walks off this hole with just a par feels like he has dropped a shot against the rest of the field. Certainly Baldovino Dassu felt that way after having five birdies in the first six holes in 1971. He went on to shoot 60 and looked back with regret at that failure to birdie the 7th. The European Tour has never come so close to witnessing its first 59.

9. Duke's Course, Woburn, Bedfordshire

Summary: Woburn returns to the European Tour schedule in 1999 and thank goodness for that. Its stately views, with virtually each hole lined by majestic trees, has been sorely missed during its five-year absence. Perhaps the highest compliment paid to Woburn came inadvertently from Laura Davies, during a time when the course was an annual host to the women's British Open. 'I love coming even though I never do very well', she said. Praise, perhaps, gets no higher. In 1996 the European Tour bought a stake in Woburn, no doubt to the delight of its members. Now it will return each year to television screens, the venue for the British Masters.

Key hole: The first hole for members is played as the 18th during tournaments, a good choice given its dramatic qualities. A long, straight par five, it offers the chance of an eagle three but out of bounds lurks to the left and the green is well protected by its front bunker. The fairway dips suddenly at one point, and can lead to some unpredictable lies. The green is generous but contains any number of subtle contours. Consequently putts over 20ft or more are rarely holed.

10. Loch Lomond

Summary: There is a strong argument for considering Loch Lomond the finest golf course built anywhere in the past ten years. Some courses acquire greatness and some have greatness thrust upon them; this one was simply born great. Built alongside the loch from which it takes its name, it makes full use of its majestic setting. In 1996 it hosted the inaugural Loch Lomond Invitational tournament and to say the players were impressed is an understatement. Well, here's how impressed, anyway: normally the top stars don't go anywhere without a six-figure appearance fee; at Loch Lomond they turn up each July for nothing.

Key hole: There are many who believe that the architect, Tom Weiskopf, reserved the best for last. Certainly the 18th is a jaw-dropping sight, winding its way around the loch. The decision on the tee is how much to bite off to avoid running out of fairway and into a series of bunkers that police its right-hand side. Too much, of course, results in the ultimate punishment of a watery grave. The two-tiered green is no easy target either, and a bunker lies in wait on its right-hand side. In short a magnificent finishing hole.

The 18th hole at Loch Lomond

Physique

It used to be one of rugby's proudest boasts: that when it came to playing the game it was a true democracy. It did not matter how big or small you were, or whether you were fat or thin – there was a position on the pitch that was perfect for you. Now, in these days of professionalism, the principle hardly applies. Few players cross the white line on to the rugby pitch unless they are strong and tall.

And so golf might be the last major sport that fits this democratic philosophy. True, more and more players are adopting the Nick Faldo attitude to the game, that a healthy body and a balanced diet lead to healthy ball striking and correct scoring. But, as the old song says, it ain't necessarily so.

As I write this, the best young player in Europe is Lee Westwood, who, without being unkind, is not what you would call a perfectly honed athlete. To exaggerate the point, Craig Stadler won the Masters in 1982 when he was four stones overweight. A lot of players, like Darren Clarke and Ernie Els, like to down a few beers when the time is right.

Furthermore, Ian Woosnam and Faldo have both reached the pinnacle in European golf and one measures 5ft 4in and the other 6ft 3in. The tallest player on the US Tour is Phil Blackmar at 6ft 7in, a whole 14 inches above Craig Parry. Blackmar weighs close to 250lbs, which makes him fully 100lbs heavier than Jeff Sluman.

For many years the perfect height and weight for a golfer was considered to be 5ft 9ins and eleven and a half stones. Tom Watson fitted these measurements to a tee. All of the above shows this no longer applies. Most of the top golfers are now around the 6ft mark. A recent survey on the US Tour showed that 54 players measured 6ft 2in or over. You can be too tall, however. Faldo has often complained throughout his career that God gave him legs that were simply too long. Longer legs translate into a leg action through the ball that is more difficult to control. Still, it never did Faldo much harm when all is said and done, did it?

The point to all this is that when you're watching golf on television and you see a pint-sized player dressed badly with an expanding midriff, don't automatically write him off against Joe tall and lean, complete with shirt that stresses his rippling torso. If you want further proof, simply tune into women's golf every now and then and watch Laura Davies slug it out against Annika Sorenstam. It should not be a contest. Davies looks as if she should simply be able to overpower the svelte Swede. The record books show, however, that this is very much a tussle of equals; indeed Sorenstam has won the women's greatest prize, the US Open, on two occasions as against Davies's one.

The Swing

Just as it is important to become quickly disabused of the notion that physique carries much weight in golf, so the same goes for how a player swings the club.

This is an aspect of the sport that always makes me howl when I am watching on television. The analysts like Alex Hay and Ewan Murray break down the swings of all the players and tell you who's stylish and who isn't, whose backswing is up to scratch these days and whose follow through is a bit dodgy. All very illuminating up to a point and yet what they are saying really doesn't add up to a hill of beans. There is only one part of the swing that matters and that is at impact. How you arrive at the point of impact and what happens thereafter is totally irrelevant alongside that overwhelmingly vital millisecond when club makes contact with ball. You can have the purest backswing you can find: if the clubface is not square to the ball at impact then it is simply there for show.

Perhaps the finest example of this ultimately meaningless style of commentary came at the 1991 Open at St Andrews. In the third round Paul Broadhurst came under the Alex Hay microscope. What happened next is perhaps best described by Broadhurst himself: 'I saw it when I got home and could not believe it. He was telling me that this was not quite correct and that could be better. I felt like yelling at the television screen: "I must be doing something right."' Indeed, he was doing plenty right. Broadhurst, on the day when Hay was ruminating on his technical deficiencies, was in the process of demolishing the Old Course with a 63, thereby equalling the lowest score ever seen in a major championship.

In 1991 they asked all the US Tour professionals who among them had the best swing. Who came top? Have a guess for a moment: as a reminder, this was when Faldo and Greg Norman were in their prime; Ian Woosnam was tearing it up in Europe; and Severiano Ballesteros was not 100–1 to win a major championship.

The answer was actually none of these, indeed I would place a small wager that you could sit in your comfy armchair all evening and still not guess correctly. It was – wait for it – Tom Purtzer. His performance sheet since eloquently shows that a great golf swing wins you nothing but plaudits.

While poor old Purtzer has been struggling to keep up, among the professionals who have passed him is Jim Furyk. If Ewan Murray or Alex Hay saw Furyk on a practice ground at a municipal golf club, practising his swing before actually hitting the ball, I'm sure they would advise him to go straight to the local pro for some lessons. In 1997 this same Furyk made over £1 million in prize money and defeated Faldo in the singles matches in the Ryder Cup.

So lesson number two, following the resistance of the temptation to judge a golfer on how he looks, is temper the desire to award too many marks for style.

All in the Mind

It is now accepted that most top-class sport, even essentially aerobic pursuits like tennis and football, are played out in the four inches between the ears. In golf it is virtually all played out in the mind. No golfer, no matter how gifted, can compensate for any major flaws in his mental make-up. Swing, yes. Physique, yes. Mental approach, no.

A prime example of this came in the 1989 Open Championship at Royal Troon. On the final day Greg Norman was performing at the height of his considerable powers. He birdied each of the first six holes in his last round and eventually came in with a 64. From well down the field, he had forced a four-hole play-off against Mark Calcavecchia and Wayne Grady. Norman birdied the first two holes of the play-off but then bogeyed the third and, with Calcavecchia birdieing the second, the pair stood on the final extra hole, the 18th, all square.

It was here that Calcavecchia, despite being technically inferior, outthought his rival to win the title. A bunker guards the right-hand side of the fairway at the 310-yard mark. Calcavecchia knew he would almost certainly not win if he went in there. It affected his thought processes badly enough that he sliced his drive wildly to the right.

Norman, meanwhile, never gave the bunker a second thought. He simply wanted to hit the ball as straight and as far as he could, to give himself the best possible advantage. He drove it far, all right, but from the moment Calcavecchia saw it take one slightly unkind hop to the right he knew that Norman was dead and buried in the bunker, and that his own badly sliced drive was now suddenly not so bad at all.

Major championships are invariably decided at moments like these. Over the final holes it is the player who is thinking clearly who usually prevails. This is why experience is such an important factor when it comes to the Grand Slam events.

Studying the faces of the leading competitors when the pressure is at its most intense is an invaluable guide to how they are thinking. You can often tell who is concentrating hard and is confident in what they are doing. The nervous ones, the players unsure of the situation in which they find themselves or whether they can trust their swings, inevitably betray their emotions.

From behind the ropes at the 1996 Masters, Nick Faldo's coach, David Leadbetter, watched Norman unravel in the final round and lose a six-stroke lead. 'I could tell, early on, that his routine was different', he explained. 'He was much quicker than usual, as if he wanted to get the shots over with.'

The difference with Norman at the 1993 Open at Sandwich was quite palpable. There he had every confidence in what he was doing; he was fully in control of his actions. Norman believed in his heart that no one could beat him that day and so it proved. The result was a final round of 64, perhaps the best final round, indeed, ever played by any competitor in a major championship.

So, how could Norman go from that state of grace in 1993 to complete disaster at Augusta just three years later? A million imponderables could have brought it about. Norman is only human, whatever his supporters may claim for him and like the rest of us he wakes up feeling better on some days than others. Pressure affects players in different ways. Was he worried about the fact he had never won a major championship before in America and this represented a golden chance? Was it the thought of winning the Masters, a tournament at which he had endured heartbreak before, and which he wants to win above all others?

Furthermore, in golf, it is important to remember that fractions can make all the difference, and explain why it is so difficult for one player to dominate. A putt that goes round the hole and drops, for example, against one that spins out, can have a dramatic effect on the confidence of a player. A pimple of land on the fairway can grotesquely divert what appeared a perfectly good drive into an awful lie in heavy rough. 'Golf was never meant to be a fair game', Jack Nicklaus once famously remarked. And so it isn't.

How can a player arm himself against the game's capricious nature? It is here that the comments of Hay and Murray make most sense. By making himself the best he can possibly be technically and by working hard on the practice ground, a player gives himself the best possible chance of combatting the forces of luck and fate that may seek to conspire against him.

In 1983 Nick Faldo was a contender for major championships but still had much to learn. Most analysts agreed that it was simply a learning process. Faldo disagreed. He felt his swing was too loose and would unravel under pressure. He took it apart piece by piece and rebuilt it. The process took over two years and during that time his performances suffered and he took a hefty barrage of criticism.

Nick Faldo

No one can dispute now that he was right. Over the last eleven years Faldo has proven himself the best player in the game with regard to being in control over the final stages of major championships. Clearly there is an innate gift but the foundation upon which it is built is the absolute belief that his swing will now stand up under pressure.

The Swing: Four Case Studies

Ernie Els v Jim Furyk: The Sublime v the Ridiculous

Ernie Els is the son of a man who owned a haulage company. Jim Furyk is the son of a professional golfer.

So when told that one has a swing that flows like liquid gold and the other like an octopus stuck in a telephone booth, you would naturally assume Furyk is the golden boy and Els the one who is all arms and legs. It is, of course, the other way around.

Who has got it right? Given that they were born within nine months of one another, and Els has a list of achievements as long as his arm and, well, Furyk has not, you would have to say that technique will out. But Furyk is enjoying a distinguished career, and has certainly achieved enough to demonstrate that it is not necessary to please all the purists to do well in golf. Sometimes instinct is a more powerful ally. By the time Furyk had made his unusual swing effective and successful it could have been fatal to tear it up and start again. Where the two players are similar is in their approach to the game and in the hitting area. The fact that both are successful demonstrates that when weighed against those two attributes, an aesthetically pleasing swing does not add up to much at all.

Fred Couples v Jose-Maria Olazabal: Slow Rhythm v Fast

The importance of rhythm in a golf swing cannot be over-emphasised: tune in to any television broadcast and you can be sure that at some point over the course of an hour a commentator will look at one player and talk about his rhythm.

Watching Fred Couples and Jose-Maria Olazabal swinging a golf club one could be forgiven for wondering what everyone was on about. One player swings the club so slowly on the backswing you could almost fall asleep watching him. The other swings it so fast you're tempted to shout out: why don't you slow it down to a blur? Yet both must be right, because both have won the Masters. What is so important about rhythm?

The importance lies not in the tempo but in finding a rhythm that is most suitable to the player concerned. Couples could not swing the club like Olazabal or, with his suspect back, he would end up in hospital. In turn, if Olazabal swung the club like Couples, with his small frame, he would hit the ball about 190 yards from the tee.

John Daly v Nick Faldo:
The Natural v the Mechanical

John Daly is golf's equivalent of Babe Ruth. 'Grip it and rip it' is his philosophy, and he more than lives up to it. By the time he finishes winding up his backswing, most players have already completed their follow through. It is the sort of swing that no golf guru would dare teach.

John Daly

Nick Faldo had a flowing swing once. He dismantled it. Now there are as few moving parts as possible. Faldo thought his old swing fell apart under pressure and the wisdom of the change is obvious whenever he looks at the six major championship mementoes that hang proudly in his trophy cabinet. Yet Daly's swing works for him under pressure as well. He has been in contention in two majors and won both of them.

If success is everything, however, Faldo's swing is clearly the more proficient. But for Daly it isn't. Daly has more people watching him on the practice ground than Faldo has watching him win the Masters.

Justin Leonard

Severiano Ballesteros v Justin Leonard:
Naivety v Practicality

Justin Leonard's swing was built to take account of the winds in his native Texas. He keeps the ball low and under perfect control. No wonder he won the Open in 1997 at a frequently windswept Troon.

Ballesteros has always had a problem controlling the ball. This problem has been exarcerbated in recent years by his muscles having atrophied down the side of his back.

Each winter the Spaniard will spend several hours a day trying to reinvigorate them but he accepts that his back is more like that of a man in his early fifties than his early forties.

The Importance of Power

One of golf's most famous sayings is: 'Drive for show, putt for dough.' Its meaning is fairly straightforward: the player who hits the ball a long way will always draw gasps of admiration from the crowd but it is the quiet genius on the greens who will collect all the money.

Clearly a lot of truth in the saying remains. No one can hope to win a major championship while having a bad week on the greens. But equally, in this age of modern technology, the ability to hit the ball a long way has become much more of an asset.

Most courses now measure over 7,000 yards for professional tournaments and most of the time the flags are tucked in difficult places, such as behind bunkers. Here is where power comes into its own. It is not the fact that Tiger Woods is fifty yards further down most fairways than every other player that gives him his massive advantage; it is that he has a wedge in his hands rather than a seven iron.

At Augusta in 1997 this was seen to its greatest effect. With the greens hard and the pins generally placed on small plateaus with little margin for error, Woods had a huge headstart over the rest of the field.

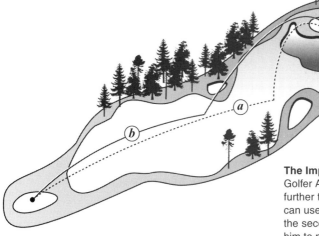

The Importance of Power
Golfer A has hit the ball further than B and therefore can use a more lofted club for the second shot. This allows him to produce backspin and stop the ball dead on the green. B has to hit and hope that his ball does not roll through the green.

The par five 15th was a particular case in point. The green here is shallow and shaped like an upturned saucer, and most players were trying to hit it with a five or six iron at best. They found that they could not impart enough spin and the ball would invariably roll through the back, leaving a difficult chip. Woods had no such problems. He had a nine iron or wedge in his hands and the greater loft meant he could spin the ball so much he could have stopped it on a sixpence.

Power is the reason why women could never hope to compete with men on an equal basis. On the greens there are a number of women professionals who can putt at least as well as the men. But not even Laura Davies can generate the power to hit down on the ball and so generate the spin that gives a top male player such control over his shots.

Power has become such an important part of the game that no professional would think of taking to the course without a metal driver in his hands. Ian Woosnam readily concedes that he does not drive the ball with metal as accurately as he once did with wood. He cannot shape the ball as well and consequently has lost accuracy. But does he ever think of going back to wood? Not a chance. He perseveres with metal. With wood he would be giving too much away to the opposition even if he recovered his accuracy. Better to keep going with metal and find a solution.

Over the years there have been short hitters who have achieved notable success. One of the best was Corey Pavin, who made up for his lack of length with a bulldog's tenacity. But how long can a player maintain such ferocious determination? Will it survive the winning of a major championship and countless millions in the bank account? And what happens when his razor sharp short game begins to fray at the edges? When these things happened to Corey Pavin, he fell off the chart.

Course Management

Not many players improve dramatically from the moment they turn professional. Colin Montgomerie is a significant exception but even notable ball strikers like Jack Nicklaus, Sandy Lyle and Tiger Woods could all propel the ball massive distances from day one as a pro. The two things they learned that turned them into champions were how to handle themselves on the course, and course management.

The golfer has various options on the tee.

a) He can attempt to drive over the trees but he may end up in the forest.

b) He can try to 'carry' the fairway bunker but he may land in it. Or he may overhit and bounce into the rough.

c) He can play an iron and 'lay up' in front of the bunker. However, from there he may not be able to see the green and will have a long, and therefore less controllable second shot.

d) He can use a 3-wood and play to a relatively safe position, although the lake is a potential hazard and the green is rather far away.

The choice he makes depends on his power, accuracy and wind direction/strength. Top professionals face these dilemmas continually and it is fascinating to watch them make their decisions.

The latter is a player's ability to plot his way around all eighteen holes. Nearly every shot involves some element of risk. Bunkers, water hazards and out of bounds are not there primarily to give a hole definition but to present a challenge. They are positioned accordingly. So, over every stroke, a decision has to be made: should I attempt to drive over that fairway bunker or should I play short with a long iron? Should I take on the water hazard with my approach, or should I lay up and pitch over with a wedge? Should I be bold with my 25ft birdie putt or settle for getting the ball next to the hole and accept a par? Assessing correctly whether a risk is worth taking on or not goes a long way to determining whether a player shoots 68 or 78.

With young professionals it is all too often the latter. They're aware of the bunker down the left-hand side that might catch their drive but there's the reckless, impatient side of youth that is sneering: 'What bunker?' Then they spy the flag and aim for it. But sometimes in golf the best play is to aim 10ft to the left of the flag not straight at it. To do so, however, can require discipline and that often comes only through bitter experience.

Augusta provides many good examples of why a player should sometimes avoid going straight for the flag. The contours of the greens are so clearly defined that to be 20ft below the hole is always better than half that distance above it. I've seen Tom Watson at the Masters hit his tee shot to the 16th to within 10ft of the hole. A good birdie opportunity, therefore? Alas, no. Watson was above the hole. The first putt missed and sped down the hill. He was 10ft away in one and 35 away in two. He ended up with a six on his card.

To be 10ft above the hole at Augusta means the putter head must barely graze the ball for the putt to have any chance of going in. Uphill is a different matter. A player can now be aggressive with his putt and apply a proper, more confident stroke.

Augusta is a course strategist's dream. At first sight it is wide open and inviting: fairways so wide they are virtually impossible to miss; no rough to worry about; greens so true that if on line you know a putt is going to disappear 6ft before it reaches the hole.

Then you start to realise that being down the right side of a fairway can leave you with no chance of getting the ball near the flag and so you are left with an almost inevitable three putt. This is the case at the 14th, where the green is like an elephant's graveyard. I remember striking a seven iron here that never left the flag for a second.

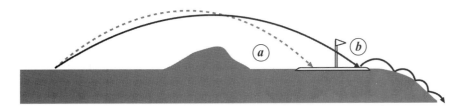

A hump was guarding the front of the green and so I could not see the ball land in relation to the flag but it seemed to me to be pretty adjacent. I was expecting hosannahs so you can imagine my consternation when the caddy said: 'Ah, bad luck.' Minutes later I knew what he meant. The ball had pitched 2ft to the right of the flag instead of 2ft to the left and instead of being close to it I was now 45ft away, since the ball had swung away on a slope. Instead of a reasonable birdie chance I was now struggling to save par. Yet the caddy had warned

Both A & B land two feet from the pin, but B bounces away down the slope. Course strategy involves knowing the contours of the green, and playing the shot accordingly.

me to make sure I was left of the flag. I was not and I suffered.

Fortunately this was simply a friendly game. But the punishment for the professionals when making an error of course management can be cripplingly high and the difference between victory and defeat.

In the 1984 Open Championship at St Andrews, Tom Watson took on the challenge presented by going for the green at the 17th hole. He had a three iron in his hands and, as he watched the ball in flight, he was convinced he had made the right decision. In fact, he had been too aggressive. His ball pitched on the green but flew over the back, over the road behind the green and against the boundary wall. With it went his chance of a sixth Open title in nine years. The mental uncertainty that such a mistake induces can be seen by the fact that Watson has not won a major championship since.

Tom Watson on the road at the 17th at St Andrews in 1984. Not the easiest of recovery shots

Three Examples of Excellent Course Management

1. Jack Nicklaus, Open Championship, St Andrews, 1970

In the 18-hole play-off against Doug Sanders, Nicklaus stood on the final tee with a one shot advantage over his opponent. What would he do now: would he just try to position a long iron or three wood and leave himself with a pitch to the green?

The 18th that day was playing downwind and Nicklaus knew that here was a risk worth taking. He knew that if he gave his three wood an almighty swing and connected properly he could probably make the putting green. The margin for error was acceptably high. If he hooked the ball he would still have a shot to the green since the last fairway at St Andrews is shared with the first and so is acres wide. In an unconsciously masterful gesture, Nicklaus removed his sweater and blasted the ball so hard it not only made the green but went through it. He then chipped down and made the putt for a birdie three that gave him the trophy.

2. Nick Faldo, Masters, Augusta, 1996

Faldo began the last round of the Masters with a six-shot deficit and the temptation must have been to try to make a series of early birdies, and be aggressive over every putt. Yet Faldo did not play that way at all. On some holes he was more than happy to accept pars. He knew that the flags would be in the most difficult places and that there would be a number of holes where par would be an eminently satisfactory score.

The Englishman shot 67 during that last round and the fact of which he was most proud was that he did not leave himself one downhill putt all day. Poor Greg Norman, the man he vanquished, left himself at least half a dozen. Still, no one could hope to make up such a leeway without attacking at some point and Faldo's masterstroke came at the 13th.

At the previous hole he had just gone ahead for the first time. Now, did he try to make the green with his second shot, knowing that if he finished in the water that protects the front of the putting surface he would hand the advantage back to Norman? It was an age before Faldo made up his mind. But once he did he showed he had the courage of his convictions, an absolutely vital ingredient of successful course management. He put the ball on the green and there was no way back for Norman thereafter.

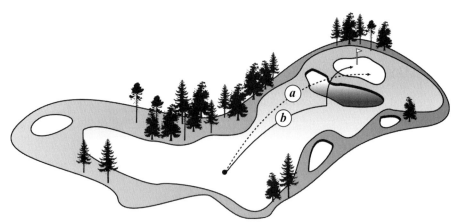

Faldo's options at the 13th. He chose A, and it was a winning stroke.

3. Ernie Els, US Open, Congressional, 1997

Coming to the 17th hole, the most difficult on the course, Els and Colin Montgomerie could not be separated. It was then that the South African showed how deeply he was thinking about the situation. He decided to take a three wood from the tee, to make sure he finished behind the Scot and so would be playing first to the green.

This was no easy shot at Congressional. Water skirts the left-hand side of the green, and the rear. Yet Els felt confident about the shot. He had played it once already that day, having completed his third round early that morning (it had been held over due to lightning the previous day). He knew he had a five iron to the target and he decided to take on the hazards, acutely aware that if he executed the shot as he wanted he would place all the pressure on his opponent.

Confidence is everything over such a stroke. It was quite a gamble but Els felt so sure he could pull it off it overrode the risk. He was right, too. The ball never left the flag for a moment, and finished 8ft away. Montgomerie later paid tribute to the blow, for he knew that his shot, difficult anyway, had been made that much harder. He pushed it, and the resultant bogey gave Els the breathing space he had been looking for.

... And Three Not So Good

1. Chip Beck, Masters, 1993

In the middle of the 15th fairway on the final day, Chip Beck, trailing Bernhard Langer by three shots, had 236 yards to carry the water that fronts the green. He knew he would need his best three wood shot to make it and he also knew that best shot was his only chance to take the green jacket from the German. Fifty yards ahead Langer, who had already laid up short, discussed the situation with his caddy, Pete Coleman. 'It's a heck of a shot to make it but I think he can do it', Langer said. 'If I was in his shoes I would go for it but I won't be unhappy if he lays up short.'

Beck laid up short, and with it went any hope of winning the Masters. It was a terrible decision, based not on the glory of victory but on the difference offered in prize money between finishing second and third. 'With hindsight perhaps I should have gone for it', Beck said lamely afterwards. There are occasions when caution simply does not have a case and this was one of them.

Jack Nicklaus and Nick Faldo were both innately cautious players when at their best. But the thing that bound them together was the instinct to know when to attack. On this occasion there is absolutely no way they would have laid up short.

2. Jesper Parnevik, Open Championship, Turnberry, 1994

Five birdies in seven holes had placed Parnevik in prime position to claim the unlikeliest of Open titles. At the time he was inexperienced with regard to the raw cauldron of emotions produced by the final nine holes of a major championship and yet he was making light of it. A par four at the final hole would surely see him out of view of his nearest challenger, Nick Price. Which is when Parnevik made his big mistake.

Nick Price celebrates his Open victory over Jesper Parnevik in 1994 at Turnberry

A glance at the leaderboard would have told the Swede that a par would have left Price needing to finish birdie, birdie simply to tie with him. He did not glance. Instead he kept on attacking, even to a pin that was cut in a tortuously difficult place. He thought he needed another birdie. Parnevik missed the green at precisely the spot which left him no chance of getting his par. Moments later Price dropped a 70ft putt for an eagle and now needed just a par at the last to win the title.

He checked the leaderboard, all right. He knew what was needed and he played for the safe half of the 18th green to secure it. What undid Parnevik that day was sheer inexperience. For the first three days of a championship a player can get away with never looking at a scoreboard. But the last day is different and particularly the last few holes. One eye should always be kept on what everyone else is doing and the strategy adapted accordingly.

3. Lee Janzen and Jim Furyk, Ryder Cup, Valderrama, 1997

Janzen and Furyk won the 17th in their foursomes match against Colin Montgomerie and Bernhard Langer and so came to the last one down as darkness began to descend. Janzen found the fairway with his drive and then Furyk the front of the green, some 60ft from the hole. As they reached their ball the light was almost gone.

Somewhere out on the course Tom Kite was moving frantically in a buggy to try to get to the scene. If he had been present, he said later, he would have told them to come back the next morning and then putt, as was their right. But Janzen and Furyk did not know this. Their instinct told them to keep going, that they had a feel for playing that might not be there in the morning. But in the gloaming they could not see that the green had been swept of water and so was playing faster than some earlier putting surfaces. Janzen's putt was practically still accelerating as it waved goodbye to the hole, eventually finishing 15ft away. Furyk could not hole the one back and so the Americans had presented the match to the Europeans.

Kite blamed it on inexperience and that was right, of course. But at least the incident appeared not to leave any lasting scars. The next day in the singles Furyk was pitted against Nick Faldo and Janzen played Jose-Maria Olazabal. Both won.

What A Difference A Day Makes

One day the wind can be docile, the sun shining, and all is well with the world. The next the wind can be a beast, the sun is well hidden from view, and the rain is striking darts at the umbrella. Every great champion who has ever played the game knows all about these two extremes; every great champion has learned how to combat them.

Actually, as strange as it may seem, a glorious day can present almost as many problems as inclement weather. On a links course that has seen hardly any rain for weeks, the turf will be like concrete and the greens fast-running. Here a player will need a touch of luck not to get any unkind bounces on the fairways; he will also need all his skill to judge how far short of the green to land the ball so that it runs out to the flag.

In bad weather, the problems are more obvious. It is here that a good caddy can really earn his money. Keeping the grips of the clubs dry is not simply desirable but absolutely essential. The game is hard enough without a club slipping in a player's hands. In wet weather the grass can get between the club and the ball in the rough and competely smother the shot.

Under these miserable conditions the good course managers invariably come to the fore. They know to play within themselves, that mistakes are inevitable, and they minimise their errors by avoiding shots that they would be lucky to pull off even in good weather conditions let alone bad.

Yet wet weather can sometimes be to a player's advantage. Ask most top golfers whether they would rather play a links course when it is dry and bouncy or when it is raining and the greens have lost their fierceness, and many would plump for the latter.

Matchplay versus Strokeplay

In strokeplay tournaments there is no real reason why a player need look at a leaderboard until the final day unless he is curious how others are playing. The requirement for the first 54 holes is simply to concentrate on his own play and try to get into contention; once there, on the last day he may choose to alter his strategy to take into account what other players are doing.

Yet there are some players who are inveterate scoreboard watchers. Colin Montgomerie is one, forever looking round for a board that will tell him how others are doing. Montgomerie uses it as a motivator, to drive himself on if others are faring much better than himself. Having said that, the Scot has another excellent game plan when it comes to strokeplay golf. With regard to what the winning score will be in a 72-hole tournament, he simply takes the leading score from the first day, doubles it, and then adds two shots. For the last three rounds that becomes his target for the week. 'It is amazing how accurate that system is, week in week out', he said.

Matchplay can be a completely different ball game, although there are some players who insist they adopt the same attitude as at strokeplay tournaments, always playing the course and never changing their approach to take into account what is happening to their opponent.

It is a baffling strategy, to say the least, and certainly not one adopted by nearly all the players who have made their names at this form of golf. Say a player is standing on the 17th tee, one up on his opponent, who has just driven out of bounds. Now it hardly makes sense to take a driver, the club he would use if he was playing a strokeplay tournament, and risk following his opponent over the boundary wall. There is no extra reward for beating your opponent by two strokes on a hole instead of one. Better, then, simply to take an iron and make sure to keep the ball in play.

Matchplay golf, if close, can be the most exciting form of the game for this reason. It contains all the basic elements of strokeplay but adds the dramatic one that a player is governed not only by his own actions but those of his opponent as well.

The Ryder Cup

For one week every two years the players who represent Europe and America at the Ryder Cup get to behave as team mates and not individuals. Actually, the Americans now get this pleasure every year since they also play a President's Cup match against the Rest of the World in non-Ryder Cup years. Given their record in recent Ryder Cups, they could clearly do with the practice.

There is no disputing that the Americans are superior players if each individual is taken in turn. But the Ryder Cup is a unique spectacle precisely because it involves the sort of principles that bind together teams and make them stronger than other sides who play simply as a collection of individuals.

At the Ryder Cup in Valderrama in 1997 Per-Ulrik Johansson played once on the first day, won – and then found himself left out completely on the second day. Ian Woosnam, Darren Clarke and Thomas Bjorn did not see any action at all until the second day.

These are tactics that the Europeans have adopted with great success in most Ryder Cups and which the Americans have never chosen to emulate. Team golf is all about subduing the ego for the good of the collective and the feeling that struck everyone who was on the Spanish coastline for three days that September is that the Europeans were much more of a team, and desired victory that little bit more.

Naturally, the quartet of Europeans did not like to be left out and Woosnam, in particular, shouted his disapproval loudly in the aftermath of the match. But which is better: to pat each other on the back in defeat, as the Americans did; or to raise bottles of champagne in victory, the happy position in which the Europeans found themselves?

Draw versus Fade

Fifty years ago most of the great players hit the ball with a draw, which gave them more distance. A draw imparted topspin on the ball, which meant that it rolled further upon landing. Over the years the players have got fitter, the balls and clubs have improved, and distance has come naturally through these other means. Consequently the fairways have got narrower to combat these developments.

In response, few players now hit the ball with a draw off the tee. The last thing they want is topspin and the risk of the ball rolling into the rough. Now most either hit the ball straight or with a slight fade, because the ball pitches softly upon landing.

There are three options here.
a) Hit through or over the trees and hope for the best. A very risky shot.
b) Chip onto the fairway. Safe, but a shot lost.
c) Draw or fade around the trees and watch the ball arc onto the green.
A difficult shot for an amateur but the professional's choice.

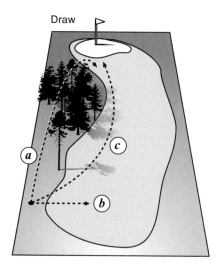
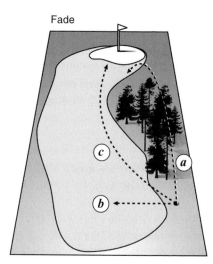

The fade is perhaps golf's least destructive shot. A draw can quickly become a hook, with terrible consequences. But it is a pretty bad shot before a fade develops into a slice.

Nevertheless, a top player still has an appreciation of all four shots: the draw and hook, the fade and slice. There will be occasions when he is blocked out by trees and needs to shape the ball around them. To fade the ball his feet will point towards the left of the target, and the club will be taken outside the normal sweep of the swing. The consequence is the blade will cut across the ball, imparting a side spin that will cause it to arc towards the right. How far a player wants it to swerve will determine how exaggerated this action will be. The opposite course of action will cause the ball to draw, or, in extreme circumstances, hook.

Severiano Ballesteros is a master of these improvised shots, indeed all improvised shots. In the Lancome Trophy in 1997 he was seemingly in a hopeless position on one hole, surrounded by trees and unable to swing properly standing up. Most players would have declared the ball unplayable and taken a penalty drop. Ballesteros dropped to his knees instead, hitting a four wood through a tiny gap in the branches. From this position he was able to swing in a much diminished arc, and as a consequence the ball never rose more than ten feet above the ground, finishing just short of the green.

The Great Players and the Shots that Help to Make Them Great

By now it will be obvious that no player can become one of the legends of the game without having a decent technique, excellent course management skills, desire, and an indefatigable spirit. It is almost an axiom that they can play all the shots in the bag. Yet it is also true that every great player has a particular shot at which he is outstanding, that rescues him time after time. Here we look at all the shots in a golfer's armoury and choose exponents in each who have developed it into an art form.

Driving: Colin Montgomerie and Tiger Woods

The driver is among a golfer's most potent weapons and the top players are invariably expert in one of two ways: they either hit the ball a long way or they are very accurate.

Tiger Woods is not among the most accurate of drivers, which places him at a distinct disadvantage on courses that hold the US Open or the USPGA Championship, since they usually have narrow fairways and are lined with heavy rough. At the Masters or the Open, however, his length is a wonderful asset. The ability to muscle a drive 75 yards past an opponent not only intimidates the opposition but means a second shot inordinately easier than the one others will face. The bad news for everyone else is that Woods is also becoming more accurate.

Colin Montgomerie

He has a long way to go, however, before he reaches the standards set by Montgomerie who, all things considered, is probably the best driver of the ball in the game today. Over the years he has added twenty yards without losing his extreme accuracy and now he is among the longer hitters. It is not a coincidence that Montgomerie has come close on three occasions to winning a US Open and once a USPGA Championship. When the rough is long and the penalty for straying into it a pitch back on to the fairway, Montgomerie's biggest asset comes into its own.

Long Irons (1–5): Jack Nicklaus

At the zenith of his powers Jack Nicklaus obviously did everything very well, but his two greatest abilities were the strongest mind the game has ever seen and an imperious quality with his long irons. Nicklaus not only had deadly accuracy with his one, two, three and four irons, he could hit them long as well. The ability to hit a one iron 230 yards as straight as a tracer bullet gave him a distinct advantage on tight par fours and also long par fives.

While most players would have to contemplate a fairway wood if they were to reach the green in two on a par five, Nicklaus could dig out a long iron and invariably the ball would find its target. For the average golfer, the idea of hitting a long iron instead of a fairway wood is anathema; the latter is far more forgiving. For the professional who can strike the long irons cleanly, there is no comparison; they offer far more control. And Nicklaus's long irons put him in control in more major championships than even his elephantine memory could recall.

Corey Pavin

Short Irons (6–9): Corey Pavin

Built like a marathon runner and with a driving distance that left him trailing Tiger Woods by something in the region of 100 yards off the tee, Pavin had to be proficient at something to survive. Around the greens he was far more than that; his short irons, meanwhile, were nothing short of brilliant. Pavin probably does have a tenner for every time he got down in two shots from 100 yards, which explains why he is a millionaire several times over. Of course it helps if you have that shot on a number of occasions in every round. A player develops a feel for it under pressure and, if he pulls it off, confidence. In the 1992 Honda Open, Pavin needed to hole a 138-yard eight iron shot to force a play-off with Fred Couples. Said Couples later: 'Normally I would have been practising my winner's speech but with Corey, from that distance in, you just never know.' You certainly don't. Pavin duly holed that eight iron shot and then won the tournament with a birdie at the second play-off hole.

Chipping and Pitching: Severiano Ballesteros

I shall always feel privileged to have watched Ballesteros and Jose-Maria Olazabal the first time they teamed up together in Ryder Cup competition. It was the first morning at Muirfield Village in 1987 and Olazabal was so nervous he later confessed that he thought he was going to be sick on the first tee. His golf betrayed his emotions. He placed his partner in positions around the greens from which no ordinary mortal would have emerged. Ballesteros's response was to conjure up a series of shots that left one shaking one's head, thinking: 'How did he do that?' It was the same at Oak Hill in the singles in 1995. Ballesteros missed every fairway and hit two greens in regulation over the first nine holes against Tom Lehman. Yet he still turned only one hole in arrears. He chipped in once and stone dead on five occasions. To be so good around the greens is a prodigious art and makes a player particularly dangerous in matchplay. The temptation when an opponent misses the green is to think you now have the advantage. With Ballesteros this is never the case. The other thing that such short game wizardry gives a player is the ability to score when he is having an off-day with his driver or long and mid-irons. And nothing instils more confidence than a miraculous escape after a particularly bad shot. Which probably explains why Ballesteros has been one of the very best players to have emerged over the past twenty years.

a) Pitch shot

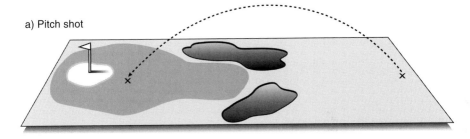

b) Chip shot

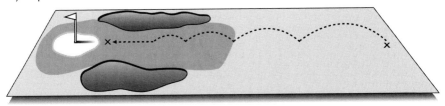

In a), a pitch is the safer option owing to the position of the bunkers. In b), a chip may be the more accurate shot. However, the decision as to which shot to use depends on the lie of the ball, firmness of the fairway, wind, roll of the green, pin placement and so on. Not as easy as it appears.

Bunker Play: Gary Player

As with Ballesteros's artistry with a pitching wedge in his hands, there is the temptation to consider Gary Player's skill from a bunker and think it innate. Certainly there is something god-given about someone who possesses such feel in their hands that they can play a touch shot with such a heightened level of skill. But equally it is not a coincidence that no one worked harder on those skills than Player or Ballesteros. Talent can only take a player so far; application is needed to finish the job. As with the player who can regularly get down in two from other shots around the greens, so the adept bunker player possesses a distinct psychological advantage. Just as his opponent eyes an opening, so the happy sand boy closes it. And Player got so good at bunker play, regularly laying the ball adjacent to the pin, that some of his opponents, frustrated beyond reason, began to get jealous. Someone who better remain nameless claimed he was lucky, never believing that anyone could be that good from bunkers. Player's reply has entered the golfing lexicon. 'Yes, I am lucky',

Gary Player blasts out of the bunker

he replied. 'And you know, the more I practise the luckier I get.' Good bunker play usually goes hand in hand with general short game excellence and just as Ballesteros can putt and play wonderfully from sand, so Player had the other two arts down pat as well. No wonder the pair are probably unrivalled as the finest matchplay performers that the modern game has seen.

Putting: Ben Crenshaw

There have been any number of great putters but if a poll was taken of those players who have competed over the last thirty years then Crenshaw would probably get more votes than anyone else. Like every other area of the game, it is not necessary to be technically pure to be good at putting; the great Japanese Isao Aoki used to have the toe of the putter head waving in the air and would break his wrists when making his stroke – supposedly the two worst sins that any putter can commit. He still got the job done. Crenshaw's stroke, however, is technically excellent, like a pendulum on a clock. Indeed, it is so good that he remains a fine putter even when he isn't using one. In the 1987 Ryder Cup singles match against Eamonn Darcy, Crenshaw was so frustrated at being three down after seven holes that he slammed his putter into the ground, broke it, and, under the rules of golf, was not allowed to replace it. So he used a one iron – and to the consternation of his opponent, starting holing, er, one irons. Three down became two, and then one. Humiliation was staring Darcy in the face but he managed to hold on for the narrowest of victories to claim glory instead. But to Crenshaw, another chapter was added to the legend of his considerable prowess regarding the game's black art.

A typical pot bunker: the 17th at St Andrews

The Tiger Economy

US Tour commissioner Tim Finchem made a landmark speech in January 1998, containing one particularly headline-grabbing sentence: 'I firmly believe that over the next few years, with regard to spectator sports on television, the big three of baseball, basketball, and football will become a big four. And the fourth sport will be golf.'

How on earth could this dramatic turn of events have materialised? Only a few years ago golf was attracting the sort of television audience that would tune in to Wimbledon v Crystal Palace on a wet Monday night. How could it now take its place towards the crowded pinnacle of sporting life? In short, the two-word answer is Tiger Woods.

Tiger Woods, a golfing phenomenon

Finchem can argue until he was blue in the face that golf audiences were rising anyway before Woods came along. But he cannot dispute the impetus that Woods's presence has given the game, and one fact alone proves it.

Woods's victory at the Masters at Augusta in 1997 was watched by half as many people again as Nick Faldo's triumph over Greg Norman the previous year. Yes, that is right. Woods's stroll in the park, an unassailable nine-shot lead at the start of the final round – normally the cue for a television ratings disaster – drew 50 per cent more people than arguably the most dramatic last day that Augusta has ever produced.

By winning his first major as a professional, in such circumstances, and – let's not skirt the issue here – by having a different complexion to practically every other golfer, Woods moved from sporting superstar to cultural icon. Suddenly his name was on front pages; tabloid newspapers wanted to know who he was dating. The fact his golfing buddies were Kevin Costner and Michael Jordan became big news. America was, still is, in thrall. In his wake the game could hardly do anything but prosper.

To cope with demand, golf courses are now being built at a rate not seen in the United States this century. When Woods returned to golf for the first time after his Masters victory, it was at the Byron Nelson Classic in Dallas. A tournament with a proud history, everyone who is anyone has played in it over the fifty-odd years it has been a US Tour event. The biggest galleries ever seen were around the 150,000 mark.

When Woods came to town, it was a 300,000 all-ticket sellout. The new audience came in their high heels, their Nike t-shirts, their mobile phones making their constant high pitch trill. Clearly some educating was needed. But the important thing for the game was that the average age of the spectators had dropped by something like twenty years in twelve months. Check-patterned trousers were nowhere to be seen.

Woods's feats have been heard around the world. Ramlan Harun, the Asia Omega Tour's executive director, was under strict orders from his children to get signed shirts from Woods when he attended the 1998 Johnnie Walker Classic in Thailand. 'Thank goodness this job allows that privilege', Harun laughed. 'All they ever thought about before Tiger came along was football. Now I would probably have been lynched if I had gone home without them.'

To think, they sneered at Nike when they agreed to pay the fledgling professional a guaranteed sum of £40 million over five years. Six months later, on Wall Street, they were saying that £100 million would have been an outrageous bargain. Good news for Nike, then, but good news for golf too, and certainly good news for Finchem. Just as Woods was emerging, Finchem was about to go into negotiations with the US television companies over a new five-year contract.

Television and Golf

The deal he came out with was fully in keeping with the game's new status. In 1998 the US Tour received £30 million a year in television revenue. By 2002, it will be £130 million. The impact on prize funds will be similarly dramatic. Finchem expects the average purse to have at least doubled to £2.5 million. Some events, like the season-ending Tour Championship, will be worth £4 million. In 1997, eighteen players became dollar millionaires simply on the strength of that year's earnings. Another four years, and the top forty will be so rewarded.

Is this healthy for golf? I see no reason to believe otherwise. It can only strengthen competition and improve standards. In other American sports, some of the outrageous salaries have alienated traditional paying customers. The baseball strike in the 1990s led to many spectators staying away from the game when the players returned, believing them to be too greedy. It is unlikely to happen in golf. For a start, there is no such thing as a salary guaranteed to a player whether he performs to his potential or simply proves a bum. If a golfer plays like a bum he earns nothing. And higher salaries for the players do not translate into higher ticket prices. It is corporate sponsorship and television that is picking up the tab.

Television in America has largely been a source for good. The game is shown every weekend on one of the three network channels and is invariably presented in a viewer-friendly two-hour package. The commentators are interesting. Even the advertisements have become more watchable, as the golf manufacturers have set their pitch at the hip and trendy and have styled them accordingly.

But can the same be said for Sky Television's coverage in Britain? True, no one could dispute that it is of the blanket variety. Practically every event on the European Tour is shown during the day and every US Tour event in the evening. Which is brilliant for the golf bore.

What, however, does it do for the casual viewer, who enjoys golf but likes a range of other sports? The analysts are almost always people who just want to talk about swings and there's rarely any wit. I fancy the response of most people is to switch to something else; the disappointing viewing figures rather bear this out.

The other problem with television coverage in Britain is that there is not nearly enough on a mainstream network. In vivid contrast to the weekly exposure in America, the BBC shows tournaments now on only seven or eight weekends a year. No wonder there are so few young people taking up the game in the UK.

The Professional Golfers' Association launch youth drives every year to attract young people but in truth it was they, in collaboration with the European Tour, who wrote a suicide note a few years ago when they gave the Ryder Cup to satellite television.

In the 1980s it was the victories in this biennial match that led to an explosion of interest in the sport in Europe. People tuned in on television and wanted to know more about this wonderful sport. What happens now? The victories are still being achieved in breathtaking style but they are now applauded merely by the converts. With no golf to watch on their television screens the young stare at their computer screens instead. Or watch some other sport.

It is impossible to overstate the importance of television in this regard. Young people who are interested in sport tune in to any game in their teenage years. Nick Faldo was a cycling fanatic with no background in golf when he happened to switch on to the 1971 Masters. 'It was the only sport on at that time of night', he explained. He was so enthralled that the following week he booked some lessons at his local golf club. What chance of capturing such people now with so little golf on the BBC?

To be fair it would be wrong to blame the European Tour alone. They have never been in the happy situation that Finchem finds himself, with all the mainstream networks competing against one another. In the UK only the BBC are interested, and even they seemed to lose heart in the late 1980s and early 1990s. Their coverage of certain tournaments was decidedly sloppy.

But to take away some events and give them instead to satellite – as the European Tour did – has had a catastrophic effect. Five years ago, the Scottish Open on the BBC was the perfect prelude to the Open, and one of the best tournaments in Europe. Then it was handed to Sky, the sponsor withdrew, and now the event is no more.

And while the sport stagnates in Britain, it mushrooms in America. The Tiger Woods Foundation has pledged to take the game to the inner cities. This is easier said than done but with the ideal totem they are exposing the game to a whole new audience. Nike's formidable backing, of course, is something more than altruistic, but they are to be applauded for their endeavours.

The Rise in Corporate Sponsorship

Given the way today's professionals are cossetted it is hard to believe that only forty years ago they were not allowed to set foot in many clubhouses. Professionals were sub-citizens, and accordingly corporate sponsorship was rare.

Now, of course, there is hardly a major blue-chip company anywhere in the world that is not involved in the game in some form or another. The car manufacturers are particularly well represented, which is fine with the players. At the Mercedes Championship in California each January, every player gets one of the sponsor's products for the week to drive around in. Mind you, it is probably less of a thrill when you're in the wonderful position of being able to go out and buy one tomorrow without a second glance at the bank balance.

When Woods won the event in 1997 and was handed the keys to a top of the range Mercedes he instantly passed them on to his mother. 'Already got one', he explained.

At the back of the US Tour's media guide there is a section called 'Marketing Partners', and it illustrates how desperate some companies are to attach themselves to golf and how the game bends over backwards to accommodate them.

Among the twenty-four marketing partners, for example, is Royal Caribbean International, the 'official cruise line of the US Tour.' Er, excuse me Mr Finchem, but why would the US Tour need an official cruise line? According to the official blurb, 'the tour sponsorship adds value to Royal Caribbean's Golf Ahoy programme, which offers guaranteed tee times on cruise/golf vacations around the world.'

What other marketing sponsors do we find? Well, there's Michelob, the official brew of the US Tour, and O'Doul's, the official non-alchohol brew. There's also Bayer Aspirins, presumably the official hangover cure for the official brew.

The appeal of the game to corporate sponsors is obvious. Many business deals are concluded over a game of golf. The sport generally attracts people with relatively high amounts of disposable income. It is free of drugs and untainted by cheating. Small wonder that in the corporate world where everyone seeks to present themselves as squeaky-clean and untarnished by scandal, it usually makes every marketing executive's shortlist.

The Game's Changing Face

The Masters is now probably the only major professional golf tournament that is not draped in sponsor's colours. Never at Augusta will you see the name of a product splashed behind a tee or a banner placed conveniently down the side of a fairway to attract a tv camera. Inside the grounds, food and drink are served from green huts that don't display the wares of any sponsor. Even the great god television is forced to bow the knee: each year CBS in America agrees to cut down on the usual number of advertisements shown during a transmission.

The other three major championships do not have overall sponsors either but the creeping hand of subsidiary donors is everywhere. Which makes the Masters a shining reminder of how the game of golf used to be.

Many people versed in the old ways of golf are appalled at this new money pouring into the game. They see today's players with a sponsor's name on the front of their shirts, another on the side, still another perhaps on the visor. 'They're not golfers anymore, they're walking billboards', one old pro loftily proclaimed. Would the old pros have been any different, given half a chance? Highly unlikely, I would suggest.

The important thing is not to compromise the game's basic integrity, and at the moment I would say the authorities are winning. But sponsors' banners behind each tee at the Open Championship and placards in places designed to attract television's all-seeing eye? It is sailing a bit close to the wind, isn't it?

The Superstars

In the wake of the rise of corporate sponsors, a new breed of superstar has followed. The television commentator Peter Alliss likens them to the movie stars of the 1930s.

In golf there are superstars and there are superstars. There are players like Colin Montgomerie, Ian Woosnam and Bernhard Langer, who have £10–30 million safely stashed away. Above them is another class, including Nick Faldo and Severiano Ballesteros, who have capitalised on their good looks as well to make up to £50 million. But above them, way above them, are three players who really do coin in money, not at the rate Humphrey Bogart or Jimmy Cagney used to, but the the way Harrison Ford and Kevin Costner do now. They are Jack Nicklaus, Greg Norman and Arnold Palmer. Of course, the world awaits what Tiger Woods will eventually earn through corporate endorsements. When he 'maximises his potential' Bill Gates had better watch out.

It was Palmer who began this trend, with the help of a then emerging sports agent called Mark

Mark McCormack

McCormack. One was a golfing genius and the other a business wizard. Thirty-five years on they are still together, still getting wealthier and wealthier. One is the most revered golfer of all time. McCormack's International Management Group (IMG) is the most powerful sports agency on the planet.

It was a fine mix. Palmer had the looks and the charisma. He took a black and white game and splashed it with colour. He appealed to the common man and McCormack exploited that appeal to the full. Even now, getting on for twenty-five years after his last success in a major championship, Palmer is still raking in more money each year than every other golfer bar Norman.

Most of his businesses are golf-related, of which the most lucrative is his course design company, which has now built more than 150 courses worldwide, including Tralee and the K Club in Ireland. Palmer's appeal, however, has always stretched outside the game's boundaries and his interests reflect this. There is the Arnold Palmer Automotive Group, for example, which runs motor dealerships in four American states (Kentucky, California, North Carolina, and his home state of Pennsylvania).

Nicklaus has fully capitalised on his position as the most successful golfer who ever lived. No player has been more active in golf course construction and there is now hardly a corner of the world in which you will not find a golf course complete with the Golden Bear logo.

Three different prospectuses are available to any potential purchaser. There is one that carries the Nicklaus name and is designed by his representatives; another where the design work is carried out by his son, Jack Nicklaus jnr; then there is the Full Monty, in which the man himself does the basic design and carries out a number of inspection visits. The work is priced accordingly, with the Full Monty into seven figures.

It is Norman, however, who has taken Palmer's example and run with it. The rugged Australian became a cultural icon in the early years of the 1990s. Now his business interests are quite staggering, and it is believed he makes upwards of £30 million every year.

Like the other two players in his income bracket, Norman is heavily involved in course design. So far he has over thirty to his name, and in 1997 one of them, Sugarloaf in Atlanta, hosted a US Tour event. Norman said it meant more to him than any other moment in his design career.

When the major championships are completed every August, Norman concentrates for four months on his business concerns. There is Norman the fashion designer, who attends shows in New York. 'So you're the new designer on the block, the man who came up with all that shark stuff', one fashion figure, who did not know him from Adam, said. All that shark stuff is now among the fastest selling leisure items in America. He has since branched out into gym wear, swim suits and women's polo shirts.

Greg Norman

Norman the restaurateur opened his first eatery in Myrtle Beach, South Carolina, in the Spring of 1998. It is called 'Greg Norman's Down Under Grill' and Norman hopes there will be 200 of them by the year 2000.

It is with two other deals, however, that Norman has shown a considerable business acumen. One involved a company called Cobra golf clubs, in which he bought a 12 per cent stake in 1991 at a cost of $1.9 million. Four years later the company was sold for $720 million, giving Norman a clear profit of over $86 million.

The other followed a call from an Australian called Hugh Whiting, who asked Norman whether he was interested in grass. 'Hell, I never even smoked the stuff', Norman replied. He was, however, wise enough to listen on.

Norman was offered a hybrid Bermuda grass that was resistant to bugs as well as being tolerant to all kinds of weather. It grows 50 per cent quicker than other grasses, which particularly interested Norman given the amount of grass that playing golf damages through taking divots.

Whiting's grass was called CT2. It is now called GN1 and can be found on all new Arnold Palmer courses, plus the baseball fields of the Atlanta Braves, with a number of American football clubs filing orders. Norman believes in time it will prove as successful as his Cobra deal.

In 1998 he took delivery of a Boeing 737 jet, completely done out inside with his own mobile office, personal gymnasium, and separate sleeping, eating, and living quarters. Norman paid for it, cash on delivery.

Modern Golfer inc:
The Business Empires of
Palmer, Nicklaus and Norman

ARNOLD PALMER
Arnold Palmer Enterprises

*Palmer Course Design Company: Over 150 courses worldwide.

*Arnold Palmer Golf Management Company: Manages 25 courses operating under the licence of Palmer Enterprises.

*Arnold Palmer Golf Academies: Due to open in late 1998.

*Ownership/management: Bay Hill Club in Florida and Latrobe Country Club in the town in Pennsylvania where Palmer was born.

*Arnold Palmer Aircraft Charter Company: Based in Chicago.

*Arnold Palmer Automotive Group: Dealerships in four states.

*Bay Hill inc: Tournament management company running the Bay Hill Invitational on the US Tour.

*Arnold Palmer Tournament Services: Provides infrastructure for golf tournaments, including the US Open.

JACK NICKLAUS
Golden Bear Inc. (public company)

*Marketing and licensing: Nicklaus clothing.

*Paragon Construction International: Builders of more than 80 courses.

*Nicklaus/Flick Golf Schools: Golf instruction centres.

*Golden Bear Golf Centres: More than 20 practice facilities.

*Jack Nicklaus International Golf Club: Affiliation

of 77 Nicklaus-designed courses.

Golden Bear International (private company)

*Nicklaus Design: 152 courses worldwide
*Golden Bear Publishing: Jack Nicklaus golf books by Ken Bowden.
*Production of televised golf events.
*Residential community development.

GREG NORMAN
Great White Shark Enterprises Inc.

*Greg Norman Course Design: More than thirty courses, including sixteen in Asia, six in America and five in Australia.
*Greg Norman Turf Company: Suppliers of GN1 grass.
*Greg Norman's Down Under Grill: Restaurant chain.
*The Greg Norman Collection: All types of leisure clothing.

Equipment

After decades where change happened with all the pace of Bernhard Langer going through his pre-shot routine, every golfer, from the world's number one to the high handicapper, now seemingly sits on the edge of his seat awaiting the latest developments in club technology.

The video of Nick Faldo's win at the 1987 Open Championship at Muirfield already looks so dated it should have been made in sepia. Young sons must look at their fathers and inquire about the odd-looking objects the players are using to hit the ball. 'Persimmon did you say Dad? That's a kind of wood isn't it?'

The magazine coverage of Faldo's victory is equally instructive. The advertisements surrounding the piece are from companies such as Dunlop, Slazenger and Wilson, which dominated the golf market for half a century but now seem like relics from a different age.

Today all three are bit players and the reasons why are not hard to find. 'Play the right clubs', announces an advertisement for Hogan clubs. 'Play our traditional irons and persimmon woods.' Such luddite thinking from the established golfing names allowed the upstart newcomers to find a niche that has since become a stranglehold.

The serious money these days is spent on products by one company in particular: Callaway. Ely Callaway did not even start the business until 1983, but the company has underpinned a change that has been every bit as fundamental as that which saw wooden shafts give way to steel in the 1930s.

Callaway's core trade has always been metal woods that were named after a First World War cannon, Big Bertha. Now we have Great Big Bertha, and the latest derivative, the Biggest Big Bertha.

The things they all offered were more distance from the tee and a greater degree of forgiveness if the ball was not struck properly; an ageing golf population snapped them up as if they were the elixir of youth itself. Callaway have always been on the cutting edge, offering titanium long before it became the industry's buzzword. In 1997, Callaway sold more than $500 million worth of metal woods alone, and in just fourteen years it has become the largest golf club manufacturer in the world.

Naturally, the Great Big Bertha comes with a great big price tag – around £400 in Britain for a single club. Well, they have to pay for Colin Montgomerie's great big contract somehow.

Yet it is not all as simple as hype. 'There are a lot of clubs out there for a lot less money and our success is solid proof of our quality and the continuing preference the public has for our products', insists Ely Callaway.

Certainly the mistakes made by other companies illustrate how quickly things can change if the products fail to deliver. Taylor Made's fortunes nosedived when it produced a series of mediocre clubs in the early years of this decade. Wilson's efforts to retrieve market share were hardly helped when its leading player at the time, John Daly, revealed he had to keep changing drivers because he was always breaking them – not quite what you want to hear when you are about to part with the thick end of £300.

But it is not just off the tee that Callaway has made an impression. Many players on the women's and senior tours now carry as many as five woods.

'I have a nine wood rather than a four iron because the greater loft means it is easier for me to get the ball airborne', explains the Swede Annika Sorenstam, the best woman golfer in the world. Similar thinking has also caused many an average player to rethink the habits of a lifetime.

What can be expected in the future? More new products, certainly. Players may have caught on that titanium-headed drivers allow them to hit the ball further with fewer degrees of hook or slice. But such is the rate of change throughout the industry it would be no surprise if titanium was not around at all in another ten years. Callaway, for example, will spend £11 million this year on research and development alone. 'When you are asking people to part with so much money for a club the secret is to continually bring new products on to the market', says an insider.

Such is Callaway's domination of that market that only Taylor Made is considered a competitor. The latter's product has improved enormously in recent years, and the company has a fine stable of contract players including Ernie Els, Mark O'Meara and Tom Lehman.

As for the older names, the manufacturers most of us grew up with, they are unlikely to move out of the margins. Dunlop-Slazenger was involved in a management buyout in 1995 and the new owners are concentrating most of their energies on Maxfli golf balls. Their time appears to have come and gone. A bit like the poor old Persimmon driver, in fact.

New Media: Computer Games, Web Sites, Simulated Golf

In 1998 on-line no longer has anything to do with an accurate drive. On-line means surfing the internet and boy, is there the opportunity for the golf enthusiast to surf. It is now possible to call up over 20,000 golf courses on the internet and check out their yardages, their specifications, even what the members are up to. All the main golf organisations now have web sites, as do many of the top players, including Tiger Woods, Jack Nicklaus, John Daly, Colin Montgomerie and Ernie Els.

Log on any morning and it is possible to know what happened in any golf tournament the day before in any corner of the world. All the facts and figures about any golfer who plays on the European Tour are available from their web site. Call up the US Tour and find out who is the leading player when it comes to hitting greens in regulation.

Another growth area is interactive computer games. Now it is possible to 'play' many of the world's great courses, like Pebble Beach in California, or Sawgrass in Florida. This form of simulation golf is improving every year, as the graphics get more realistic. It still does not come close to the real thing but on a cold winter evening it provides an alternative to Coronation Street. Or, more likely, the latest version of Doom.

A more approximate form of simulated golf is now being offered in many leisure centres. Here you do actually play golf, by striking a ball against a large screen which is showing a picture of a hole at, say, the Belfry. The screen's sensors can detect if you have hooked or sliced the shot and relay this information back to a central computer. Now the image on the screen will change: it will tell you have far you have hit the ball and whether you are in the rough, on the fairway, in a water hazard, or behind a tree. The lie you have been left with will be on the screen as will the information on how far you have to the pin, and what hazards you face.

It is as well not to analyse it too seriously, because for obvious reasons it is impossible to simulate accurately each green, or each bunker shot. But again, on cold days in winter, it has its virtues, and at least you are swinging a club.

Golf gets Hip

In the *Daily Telegraph* recently there was an article from its former editor Max Hastings in which he criticised golfers for their poor taste in clothing. Leaving aside the fact his photograph illustrated a haircut that hasn't adorned most heads since Oswald Mosley in the 1930s, where has he been these past five years?

Someone should whisper in his ear that golf apparel is now the height of trendiness. Robin Williams's classic line ('Golf is the only game where a white man can dress like a black pimp and get away with it') is now only relevant when watching old videos of Tom Watson winning the Open Championship.

Golf was once a game that clothing manufacturers like Armani, Jaeger, and Boss would not touch with a bargepole. Boss is now the official clothing sponsor for the European Tour, while Armani and Jaeger both have golfing lines, as do most of the couturiers who would have a luvvie fit if anyone showed them golf action from the 1970s. It has been some revolution.

True, there is still some way to go on the music front. Ask your average golfer who is playing on his car stereo and the usual array of depressing names come up: Chris de Burgh, Phil Collins, Eric Clapton, etc. ad nauseam.

But there is hope, even here. The American pro Tommy Tolles has not only heard of a range of musicians under the age of thirty-five, he is actively trying to educate his peers to listen to them. What a star the boy is.

Making the Game More Accessible

At the start of 1998 *USA Today* carried out a survey to find out which sport, among people under twenty-five, had become more cool over the previous twelve months. Golf did not just come top, it demolished the competition. Yet in Britain a poll conducted by Sports Marketing Surveys showed the percentage of people under twenty-five taking up the game had dropped by an alarming 30 per cent.

Now alright, it was not difficult for golf to improve its coolness to young people in America. For generation X, it had previously stood alongside weekends away with their parents in terms of desirability. It could hardly fail to rise.

But why has this not transferred across the Atlantic? Why the incredible disparity? We have already explored some of the reasons earlier in this chapter: the Tiger Woods effect for one; the absence of golf from mainstream television for all but eight weekends of the year for another.

There are other factors. In America the sport has done a wonderful job of re-inventing itself and becoming accessible. It can be compared with the way football changed in the wake of the hooliganism problem in the 1980s and became instead a sport in all-seater stadiums attended by men, women and children.

The same thing has happened in Sweden, where 20 per cent of the membership of every club has to comprise players under the age of eighteen. But in too many parts of Britain the sport remains mired in a cloistered way of thinking. Juniors are barely tolerated, locked away at weekends and only let out to play when the members are at work. Many clubs still have to be dragged into the twentieth century, let alone the twenty-first.

The former Ryder Cup captain Bernard Gallacher has seen the warning signs. 'It is a time-bomb ticking within the game', he says. 'Unless we address this issue now in the face of growing competition from other sports we will see golf in its homeland decline.'

The Golf Foundation, the national body for the development of junior golf, has launched a five-year drive at grassroots level to try to do something about the situation. It is a worthy effort. But until old men at establishment golf clubs realise the errors of their ways, as they have in America, the game will continue to lose out.

Tiger Woods v Ernie Els: World Domination at Stake

Like every other major sport, golf has always thrived on rivalries. Ben Hogan versus Sam Snead; Jack Nicklaus and Arnold Palmer; Jack Nicklaus and Tom Watson; Sandy Lyle and Nick Faldo; Bernhard Langer and Severiano Ballesteros.

Ernie Els versus Tiger Woods is shaping up to be one of the best for some time. When asked who he thought would prove the better of the two, Gary Player plumped for Els. Nicklaus was then quickly on the scene to disagree. 'Well, what do you expect?' said Greg Norman, barely able to suppress a smile. 'Jack goes for the American and Gary the South African. What a surprise!'

Norman, when pinned down, did give Els the edge, which was fair enough given that he was speaking in February, 1998. But the Australian also acknowledged that the South African was six years older and when the ages are twenty-two and twenty-eight and the sport is golf, that counts for an awful lot.

Els wins the vote from many because his swing is built to last; not for Ernie a meteoric year followed by a fallow one. There also beats the heart of a true competitor as well.

At the Johnnie Walker Classic in Thailand at the start of 1998, Els led Woods by eight shots going into the final round and lost in a sudden-death play-off. To say he was annoyed with himself is an understatement. For the next few weeks he was barely out of the top three in any tournament.

The powerful Ernie Els

Els has shown he has the game to win on any golf course, any major championship. To date, Woods has yet to find the accuracy that enables him to challenge consistently on tight, tree-lined venues.

Where he has the edge is in sheer flair. Woods has a presence that Nicklaus had: when he starts to creep up a leaderboard, there is an almost tangible sense of fear among his rivals.

His performance at the 1997 Masters, which he won by twelve shots, indicated that when at the height of his powers the rest, even Els, may as well pack up and go home. Els is long off the tee but still he is playing seven irons to greens while Woods is hitting nine irons.

Woods swings through

But if Woods cannot find the fairway as regularly, then that advantage is not only nullified but handed over to his opponent. Flair and talent are wonderful assets but wasted on the young if there is no consistency as well.

Norman believes that Woods will have to change his swing if he is to challenge for the next twenty years. At twenty-two the lower back feels no strain; at thirty-five it is a different matter if precautions are not taken when young. Poor Severiano Ballesteros is testament to that.

When asked about Woods, Els could hardly have been more complimentary. 'He has raised the bar, and everyone is working harder to keep up with him as a result', he said. But he did wonder how Woods would react to a spell of poor form. 'At the moment everything is fired by self-belief. What will happen when he realises that sometimes the wonder shots not only don't always come off but end in disaster?'

It is a good point, for Ballesteros, golf's last boy wonder, was never the same player after he lost the 1986 Masters through his own errors and he realised that it was not, after all, *destino* (destiny) that won major championships.

For his part, Woods pays due credit to Els's wonderful temperament. 'It is a fantastic gift to be able to stay calm when things go wrong', he acknowledges.

Woods versus Els? I have no doubts that Woods will prove wrong those who believe him a meteor whose career will burn out. But Els is going to continue to win more than his fair share of majors too. Golf is lucky to have both of them.

Eight Other Modern Heroes for the New Millennium

David Duval

1. David Duval: Some players, when they learn how to win, never stop winning. Duval took this theory and exploited it to the full. He played eighty-six events on the US Tour and the best he achieved was a growing succession of near misses. Then he won three tournaments in a row at the back end of 1997 and followed it up for good measure with an early success in 1998. At the same time Duval went in for a lifestyle change as well. Hitherto stocky bordering on fat, he lost 20lbs, grew a fashionable goatee beard, and now walks round in sponsored Tommy Hilfiger clothes. There is no reason to suppose that having made the big breakthrough he will not stick around. His swing is textbook smooth and once he starts making some birdies in a round he never seems to stop. He looks as comfortable at the Open as he does at the US Open. If anyone is to challenge the hegemony of Woods and Els, this 26-year-old from Jacksonville is currently the boy most likely.

Lee Westwood

2. Lee Westwood: It is a great gift to be able to get over the first flush of success, to have the cars, the house, the seven figures in the bank, and still come back hungry for more. So far, Westwood has emerged from temptation with his desire intact. There's certainly the game there to ensure a European presence among the next generation. Modern golfers depend upon power and Westwood marries it with accuracy to produce a potent weapon. Then there's his temperament, which Tiger Woods is on record as admiring. So far he has shown himself a big-match player. On his debut at the Masters in 1997, paired with Jack Nicklaus, Westwood went over and consoled the great man when he started badly and told him he was sure things would get better. At the end of the year, he defeated Greg Norman in a play-off for the Australian Open. 'I like play-offs', he said. 'After all, the worst thing that can happen to you is that you will finish second.' Perversely, it is the golfer who can bring that sort of relaxed approach to play-offs who so often finishes first.

3. Justin Leonard: A throwback to a different age, when all golfers had short back and side haircuts. Leonard's life is as orderly as his swing: everything is arranged neatly in his bachelor flat in Dallas. It is said that in his sock drawer all pairs are laid out, side by side, and woe betide anyone who messes with this well-observed tidiness. Leonard's idea of a wild night on the town is probably a trip to the rodeo. Beneath that placid exterior, however, is some competitor. If his victory in the 1997 Open was a surprise to some then a runners-up finish in the following USPGA Championship should have disabused many of the notion that his earlier triumph was somehow a fluke. Leonard's one problem in years to come will be how to compensate for a relative lack of power. At present he overcomes it with tenacity, accuracy and a wonderful touch around the greens. Gary Player managed to preserve these qualities through four decades to remain a true competitor. Leonard will have to do the same if he is to remain a contender.

4. Phil Mickelson: It may seem a harsh thing to say about someone who has won more than a dozen tournaments on the US Tour before the age of twenty-seven but Phil Mickelson should have achieved a whole lot more by now. Only Tiger Woods can match him for natural talent, and even he has to bow the knee around the greens. But something remains missing between the ears of Mickelson and until he can find the answer the world will remain in thrall only to Woods and Els. I suspect one major championship would give him the self-belief to join the aforementioned pair in a big three to match the one we saw in the 1960s: Player, Palmer and Nicklaus. But one major remains a move upwards that Mickelson has so far been unable to make. Still, let us not be too harsh. To be under thirty with looks and talent to burn is a wonderful combination. And the most wonderful thing about it is if Mickelson truly desires it, it can only get so much better.

Phil Mickelson

5. Ignacio Garrido: Sons of Ryder Cup players are rare enough but those who go on to surpass the achievements of their fathers are a decidedly select species. Ignacio Garrido, whose father Antonio partnered Severiano Ballesteros in the first match in which the continentals were assimilated to make a true European Ryder Cup side in 1979, is one such person. Garrido, from Madrid, is just twenty-five and blessed with a serious dose of ambition. At the 1997 Ryder Cup he demonstrated that he has the temperament to match, forming a fine combination with Jose-Maria Olazabal that yielded 1.5 points out of two.

Sometimes it is one shot that can single out a player and so it was in this instance, a bunker shot at the 17th that showed such nerve and skill that even the watching maestro Severiano Ballesteros would have been hard pressed to have emulated it. His opponent Phil Mickelson, another noted sand exponent, was so stunned that he missed a straightforward 6ft putt.

6. Stewart Cink: Three Nike Tour victories, two children, one US Tour win; you could say Stewart Cink, at twenty-four, is a fast worker. Here's one player who earned his credits the difficult way, getting his card by virtue of that hat-trick of victories on the second-tier circuit.

Cink was married while still at college, a father at 20, and money had to be tight. But a little struggle never did any great player any harm and will surely aid Cink in the long term. And money is no longer tight, having earned over $1 million in his last two seasons. Great golfers are usually not as tall as 6ft 4ins, but Cink's attitude will help him combat any problems.

In his rookie season in 1997, having been named the Nike Tour player of the year in 1996, Cink showed no sense of being in awe at his new surroundings, eventually finishing 31st on the money list with over $800,000 earned. This is one Cink who has definitely learned how to swim.

7. Thomas Bjorn: Four down after five holes to the Open Champion usually spells a resounding defeat in Ryder Cup competition. Thomas Bjorn forced a half against Justin Leonard in the 1997 matches at Valderrama. It was quite a performance, a testament to his power and talent and Severiano Ballesteros, for one, believes Bjorn has it within him to go on to become one of the best players in the world over the next decade. If he does it will be quite something given his background, for Denmark and golf go together like a fish and a bicycle.

But there's a competitor there, illustrated not only by that showing against Leonard, but a few months later when he realised that he was the only 1997 Ryder Cup player who would not be at the following year's Masters. Bjorn responded to the terrible insult in the best way possible: he won his next tournament, the Heineken Classic in Australia.

8. Sergio Garcia: What do you mean you haven't heard of him? Alright, I'll come clean, this is a bit of a flier, partly based on Spain's wonderful record of producing outstanding young talent. And Garcia, just eighteen, has a record to live with the best of them. In 1997 he emulated Olazabal in winning the British Boys' Championship and then followed up by demolishing the field in the Spanish Open Amateur Championship.

In his native land they're already calling him the new Ballesteros, the new Olazabal. Well, as long as their expectations are not too high, that's ok then.

The Future: A World Tour?

To those outside the sport it must seem amazing that here we are, on the cusp of the new millennium, and golf has no World Tour as such. Why ever not, for goodness sake, in these days when getting anywhere is a relatively simple task, when all the players can easily afford Concorde or first-class travel, when six different countries are represented among the world's top eight golfers? Why does the game not have a circuit such as they have in equivalent sports like motor racing and tennis?

Certainly it would be more exciting if, each week, all the best players were congregated in one place; if every fortnight there was one Grand Prix event somewhere on the globe with accumulating World Championship points.

Alas, it will not happen and the reason is the established position of the tours already in place: the US, European, South African, Australian and Japanese Tours. For the leading officials of all these tours, there is too much to lose.

If, say, all the best players were in Australia one week, who would want to sponsor the event running opposite it in Europe, featuring all of the perceived flotsam? Besides, the US Tour is more than happy with things as they stand. Most of the best players compete there anyway and, with enormous increases in prize money on the way over the next few years, that situation will only continue.

For those who would like to see all the best players in one place in more events than just the

four majors and the Players' Championship in
Florida each March there are, however, exciting
developments in the pipeline.

In 1999 the professional game will slightly
change tack with the introduction of three World
Championship of Golf events, two in America and
one at Valderrama. This is the response of the
established professional tours to try to head off
anyone starting a World Tour.

The first of the three events is the one that will
intrigue the most people, a matchplay tournament
featuring the top 64 players in the world. That will
take place at La Costa, San Diego, in February.

In August, the format for qualifying for the World
Series at Firestone will change. Now it will
feature those players who have played in the most
recent Ryder Cup and President's Cup matches.
The third event, at Valderrama in November, will
be a strokeplay tournament. A fourth competition,
a team event replacing the World Cup, will be
added in 2000.

The changes will help strengthen the US Tour in
February, a time when it is traditionally at its
weakest, and extend the run of good tournaments
through to the Masters each April. The event at
Firestone will come a fortnight after the USPGA
Championship and so add something to the period
between that event and the Ryder Cup. While the
strokeplay tournament will help strengthen the
end of season programme in Europe. Thus, golf
will become a ten-month game between February
and November each year.

No doubt in December and January there will still

be some events like the Sun City Challenge in South Africa that will continue to attract fields on account of large first prizes. But the appeal of such tournaments will surely be diminished in time given the huge amounts of prize money these new tournaments will offer.

Furthermore, a two-month break each year would be good for the game, to rekindle everyone's interest rather than a sport that seems to drag on all year round.

The Future:
Ten Alternative Predictions for 2020

1. The European Tour visits thirty-five different countries on four different continents: America, Australia, Asia, and India.

2. A young Russian golfer emerges and declares that he is after Tiger Woods's record of 22 major championships.

3. Five years before Woods reaches the US Senior Tour and already officials are predicting that prize money will reach $1 billion.

4. Jack Nicklaus concedes that he is no longer competitive in the major championships but wants to have one more shot at winning the Open.

5. Nick Faldo's son, Matthew, a struggling European professional, complains about his treatment at the hands of the British press.

6. Bernhard Langer's son Stefan breaks the European Tour record by taking seven hours to complete a round.

7. The Old Course at St Andrews is lengthened to 8,000 yards to take into account the latest developments in new technology.

8. Woods buys the latest rocket on the market, cutting down travel time between Britain and America to one hour.

9. Nick Faldo's daughter Georgia, a strong player on the LPGA circuit, complains about her treatment at the hands of the British press.

10. Baldomero Ballesteros wins the Open. His father, Severiano, floods St Andrews with his tears.

Fourball: Usually only seen in televised tournaments at the Ryder Cup. It is a format that can lead to some spectacularly exciting scoring, since two players combine to form a team, with their best score on each hole counting.

Foursomes: Often referred to in America as alternate shot, which certainly gives a clearer idea of the format. Again two players form a team but this time just one ball is in play, each player striking it in turn. The player who drives off on one hole, however, will not drive off on the next, even if his partner took the last putt on the previous green.

Greensomes: Here both players drive off on every hole, before choosing the ball they consider best placed. They then proceed as in the foursomes format.

Stableford: Liked by many humble amateurs, since it enables a player to have a nightmare on a hole without wrecking his card. An eagle gains a player four points on a hole, a birdie three, a par two, a bogey one, and a double bogey or worse no points at all. The system was invented in 1931 by Dr Frank Stableford from Wallasey, Merseyside. A bastardised form of it is used in the International tournament, held each August on the US PGA Tour. Here, five points are awarded for an eagle, two for a birdie, nothing for a par, minus one for a bogey and minus three for a double bogey.

Skins: An American form of the game. Players compete against each other for money on every hole; if a player wins the hole outright, he wins a skin; if two or more players are tied for the best score, the stakes are carried over to the next hole, and so on. A Skins game is held at the end of each season in America and four of the top stars compete for lots of dollars in a television extravaganza that always pulls in huge ratings.

The Major Championships

The Masters		
1960 Arnold Palmer	1973 Tommy Aaron	1986 Jack Nicklaus
1961 Gary Player	1974 Gary Player	1987 Larry Mize
1962 Arnold Palmer	1975 Jack Nicklaus	1988 Sandy Lyle
1963 Jack Nicklaus	1976 Raymond Floyd	1989 Nick Faldo
1964 Arnold Palmer	1977 Tom Watson	1990 Nick Faldo
1965 Jack Nicklaus	1978 Gary Player	1991 Ian Woosnam
1966 Jack Nicklaus	1979 Fuzzy Zoeller	1992 Fred Couples
1967 Gay Brewer	1980 Severiano Ballesteros	1993 Bernhard Langer
1968 Bob Goalby	1981 Tom Watson	1994 Jose-Maria Olazabal
1969 George Archer	1982 Craig Stadler	1995 Ben Crenshaw
1970 Billy Casper	1983 Severiano Ballesteros	1996 Nick Faldo
1971 Charles Coody	1984 Ben Crenshaw	1997 Tiger Woods
1972 Jack Nicklaus	1985 Bernhard Langer	

1986

The newspaper cutting said it all: Jack Nicklaus is forty-six, all washed up, and for the first time for twenty-five years will not be a factor at the Masters. So Nicklaus neatly cut it out and pinned it to the refrigerator door of the Augusta home that he was renting. It was all the motivation he needed for one glorious last hurrah as, on a never-to-be-forgotten Sunday afternoon, a new generation witnessed the awesome power of Nicklaus at his best.

He started the final round four shots behind Greg Norman and, after seven holes, he was further adrift. Nicklaus then went birdie-birdie-birdie-bogey-birdie-par-eagle-birdie-birdie. One by one the people ahead of him on the leaderboard melted away amidst the onslaught. No one was happier than the writer from the *Atlanta Constitution* who contentedly gorged on humble pie.

1987

Just as they had in 1986 Greg Norman and Severiano Ballesteros were vying for the title. Just like the previous year, a supposed no-hoper stood in their way. This time it was not a legend perceived to be on the way down but a journeyman who had never been all the way up. But Larry Mize still made the three-way sudden-death play-off with the other two. At the first extra hole, the 10th, it was Ballesteros who dropped out, shedding many tears as he walked back up the steep hill. At the 11th, Mize missed the green: now surely Norman would win, for the chip appeared a terribly difficult one to get close. Mize, the local boy, who used to climb up Augusta's fence to peer at its immaculately lawned acres, played the shot to perfection. It bounced correctly on the humps, took the borrows he imagined, and disappeared into the hole. A few months later, for a magazine article, he tried the shot one more time. In twenty attempts he never came close.

THE UNITED STATES OPEN		
1960 Arnold Palmer	1973 Johnny Miller	1986 Ray Floyd
1961 Gene Littler	1974 Hale Irwin	1987 Scott Simpson
1962 Jack Nicklaus	1975 Lou Graham	1988 Curtis Strange
1963 Julius Boros	1976 Jerry Pate	1989 Curtis Strange
1964 Ken Venturi	1977 Hubert Green	1990 Hale Irwin
1965 Gary Player	1978 Andy North	1991 Payne Stewart
1966 Billy Casper	1979 Hale Irwin	1992 Tom Kite
1967 Jack Nicklaus	1980 Jack Nicklaus	1993 Lee Janzen
1968 Lee Trevino	1981 David Graham	1994 Ernie Els
1969 Orville Moody	1982 Tom Watson	1995 Corey Pavin
1970 Tony Jacklin	1983 Larry Nelson	1996 Steve Jones
1971 Lee Trevino	1984 Fuzzy Zoeller	1997 Ernie Els
1972 Jack Nicklaus	1985 Andy North	

1960

It has been called the most exciting major championship of all time. It was certainly epochal. In contention on the final day stood three players at various crossroads in their careers. There was Ben Hogan, representing golf's past; Arnold Palmer, the current hero; and Jack Nicklaus, its future. In their different ways they all lived up to the symbolism. Thirty-six holes were played on the final day and Hogan hit no less than thirty-four consecutive greens. But his putting had gone by now and he scored far worse than he deserved. Arnold Palmer, as befitted the current golden boy, shot the winning score of 280. While in the clubhouse afterwards, a disappointed Hogan spoke a prophetic sentence: 'I played 36 holes today with a kid called Nicklaus who should have won this thing by ten strokes.'

1966

Six years on from one of his greatest triumphs, Palmer was to suffer a defeat that would haunt him his entire career. Seven ahead with nine to go, six in front with six holes to play, Palmer made the fatal mistake of thinking the tournament won, and started to concentrate on the record score of 276. Five pars and a bogey would have given him 275. Palmer then went bogey-par-bogey-bogey-bogey and found himself in an 18-hole play-off against Billy Casper. The next day Palmer shot 73 against Casper's 69. It is perhaps tough on Casper that the tournament is remembered for Palmer's collapse. It was not just Palmer's bad golf that made a remarkable story-line come to pass but Casper's inspired play as well. He hit every fairway on that back nine, missed just one green, and played the holes in just 32 shots.

THE OPEN CHAMPIONSHIP

1960 Kel Nagle	1972 Lee Trevino	1985 Sandy Lyle
1961 Arnold Palmer	1973 Tom Weiskopf	1986 Greg Norman
1962 Arnold Palmer	1974 Gary Player	1987 Nick Faldo
1963 Bob Charles	1975 Tom Watson	1988 Severiano Ballesteros
1964 Tony Lema	1976 Johnny Miller	1989 Mark Calcavecchia
1965 Peter Thomson	1977 Tom Watson	1990 Nick Faldo
1966 Jack Nicklaus	1978 Jack Nicklaus	1991 Ian Baker-Finch
1967 Roberto de	1979 Severiano Ballesteros	1992 Nick Faldo
Vicenzo	1980 Tom Watson	1993 Greg Norman
1968 Gary Player	1981 Bill Rogers	1994 Nick Price
1969 Tony Jacklin	1982 Tom Watson	1995 John Daly
1970 Jack Nicklaus	1983 Tom Watson	1996 Tom Lehman
1971 Lee Trevino	1984 Severiano Ballesteros	1997 Justin Leonard

1969

There is nothing better than seeing a young man fulfil all his potential and for Tony Jacklin, that moment came on a glorious summer's evening at Royal Lytham and St Annes. Not since 1951 had a British player won the Open but the wait ended memorably following one of the most acclaimed drives that any player has ever struck. The 18th at Lytham requires an artist's precision at the best of times; when it is the last hole of an Open, it can be the most nerve-wracking of experiences. For Jacklin, however, this was his finest moment, a 300-yard shot that never looked like ending in any of the bunkers that make the drive such a difficult proposition. When he followed it with a seven iron into the middle of the green, all Britain celebrated as rarely before or since. Truly, a people's champion.

Tony Jacklin after the 1969 Open

1984

To win the Open is always the goal of any professional but to win it at St Andrews must represent the ultimate ambition. Imagine, therefore, how Tom Watson felt in 1984, a winner of five Opens already on five different courses, but never a champion at St Andrews. And now he had his chance. Level with Severiano Ballesteros playing the 17th, if only he could force a birdie, force his opponent's hand. Having won all his Opens in an eight-year period Watson must have felt imperious; in any event, the shot he tried to play suggested as much. He paid the ultimate price for his boldness, the ball scurrying through the green and to the boundary wall. The result was a bogey. Up ahead, at almost the same moment, Ballesteros was holing from 20ft for a birdie. For once the smile on Watson's boyish face was replaced by a grimace. The glory belonged to Ballesteros and how he seized the moment: a matador's thrust of joy to all the spectators, who recognised one of the great moments with a tumultuous roar.

THE USPGA CHAMPIONSHIP

1960 Jay Herbert	1973 Jack Nicklaus	1986 Bob Tway
1961 Jerry Barber	1974 Lee Trevino	1987 Larry Nelson
1962 Gary Player	1975 Jack Nicklaus	1988 Jeff Sluman
1963 Jack Nicklaus	1976 Dave Stockton	1989 Payne Stewart
1964 Bobby Nichols	1977 Lanny Wadkins	1990 Wayne Grady
1965 Dave Marr	1978 John Mahaffey	1991 John Daly
1966 Al Geiberger	1979 David Graham	1992 Nick Price
1967 Don January	1980 Jack Nicklaus	1993 Paul Azinger
1968 Julius Boros	1981 Larry Nelson	1994 Nick Price
1969 Raymond Floyd	1982 Ray Floyd	1995 Steve Elkington
1970 Dave Stockton	1983 Hal Sutton	1996 Mark Brooks
1971 Jack Nicklaus	1984 Lee Trevino	1997 Davis Love
1972 Gary Player	1985 Hubert Green	

1984

It is one of the characteristics of the great champions that they are able to summon from somewhere the effort for one last glorious finale, long after convention had dictated that they had ceased to be capable of such heroics. Jack Nicklaus's victory at Augusta in 1986 at the age of forty-six certainly came into that category and so, too, did Lee Trevino's at the USPGA two years earlier. Trevino had largely been missing from tour life for two years owing to painful back surgery and no one expected any return to former heights at the age of forty-four. But in a compelling battle of the oldies, Trevino claimed his sixth major championship title over a gallant runner-up, Gary Player.

1986

The Grand Slam of all four major championships has, of course, never been completed. History records that Ben Hogan was the only one who came close, winning the first three in 1953. But Greg Norman achieved a sort of fame on the same subject in 1986 when he led after three rounds of all four majors – a Saturday Slam if you like. The only one he won was the Open, while at the USPGA we witnessed the frailty over the closing holes and downright ill fortune that has fatally combined to undermine him on so many occasions. Three strokes ahead with six holes to play, Norman found himself tied with the unheralded Bob Tway playing the last. It looked advantage Norman when Tway found a bunker with his approach; until, that is, Tway holed the sand shot. The following day the local paper came up with a cruelly precise title for Norman, culled from a Billy Crystal film doing the rounds at the time: *Mr Saturday Night.*

RYDER CUP					
1979	Europe 11,	USA 17	1989	Europe 14,	USA 14
1981	Europe 9.5,	USA 18.5	1991	Europe 13.5,	USA 14.5
1983	Europe 13.5,	USA 14.5	1993	Europe 13,	USA 15
1985	Europe 16.5,	USA 11.5	1995	Europe 14.5,	USA 13.5
1987	Europe 15,	USA 13	1997	Europe 14.5,	USA 13.5

1991

You could say the Americans were fed up by this stage not having the Ryder Cup in their possession. Local shock jocks were employed to wake up the Europeans in the early hours; Corey Pavin wore an army cap as if he had just returned from the Gulf War; Steve Pate decided that an injury that had kept him out of the first day but not the second had returned sufficiently to prevent him from keeping an appointment with Ballesteros in the singles. In other words there was needle and aggro everywhere and it wasn't really what the Ryder Cup was supposed to be all about.

But in the end it came down to a shattering climax: Bernhard Langer, with a 6ft putt to retain the trophy. His putt appeared in the hole until the final moment, when it veered cruelly and the Americans did their jigs of joy. Ballesteros, hitherto Langer's greatest rival, told the press: 'The pressure on that putt was so great no one could have holed it. No one.' Sporting words, to relieve the situation. Not that Langer ever let anything get the better of him. The strongest mind in the modern game, he went out and won the very next week.

1995

You could also say the Europeans were underdogs for this one. The American magazine *Golf Digest*, in one of the great predictions, said: 'The Ryder Cup is about to return to the days of one-sided routs.' Mind you, when Pavin closed out the second day with a chip in to give America a two-point lead going into what is traditionally their strongest suit, the singles, Europe looked as if they would be lucky to get away with a rout. Bernard Gallacher came up with some brave words. Asked about what had gone on over the first two days, he said: 'Looking back is for amateurs. Professionals always look forward.'

I bet he looks back with pride these days, however. It was one of the great fightbacks, a sensational last day that culminated with the unsung Philip Walton claiming the winning point. The poor boy has never been the same since. Credit as well, however, to a sporting American captain in Lanny Wadkins and the Oak Hill galleries who took the contest to a new level in sportsmanship. It was one of the great Ryder Cups and Wadkins and the crowd played their parts too.

EUROPEAN TOUR GOLFER OF THE YEAR		
1985 Bernhard Langer	1990 Nick Faldo	1995 Colin Montgomerie
1986 Severiano Ballesteros	1991 Severiano Ballesteros	1996 Colin Montgomerie
1987 Ian Woosnam	1992 Nick Faldo	1997 Colin Montgomerie
1988 Severiano Ballesteros	1993 Bernhard Langer	
1989 Nick Faldo	1994 Ernie Els	

USPGA PLAYER OF THE YEAR		
1985 Lanny Wadkins	1990 Nick Faldo	1995 Greg Norman
1986 Bob Tway	1991 Corey Pavin	1996 Tom Lehman
1987 Paul Azinger	1992 Fred Couples	1997 Tiger Woods
1988 Curtis Strange	1993 Nick Price	
1989 Tom Kite	1994 Nick Price	

Five Essential Golf Books

1. *Not Only Golf* by Pat Ward-Thomas

The *Daily Telegraph* is generally considered the golfer's newspaper but no paper comes close to comparing with the *Guardian* when it comes to the quality of writing from its golf correspondents. It was Pat Ward-Thomas who gave momentum to this now proud tradition, and he stands as perhaps the most underrated of all golf writers.

This is a wonderful book, full of anecdotes and acerbic comments, as the following excerpt demonstrates: 'I am neither so vain nor so stupid as to expect to hit good shots all the time. It is the difference between the moderately adequate and the ghastly that is hard to tolerate. Unlike some people I do not find the latter amusing. For instance, to smother a four wood shot from a good lie in calm air when little is at stake is unforgiveable; or to leave a straight, level putt of five feet to win a hole short on line smacks of cowardice. I have often failed to come to terms with the fact that to err is human.'

Great stuff.

2. *The Complete Book of Golf* by Michael McDonnell

McDonnell has been golf correspondent of the *Daily Mail* for over thirty-five years and he passes on the accruing wisdom with a wit and insight that made me green with envy when I read this book a decade or so ago. Writing daily reports for a tabloid newspaper, by definition, inevitably takes a reporter into the realms of personality journalism. Here, McDonnell demonstrates an equal mastery of the other side of the trade; this is a beautifully well-written book.

Mind you, McDonnell does not always get it right. He once gave away a prototype putter given to him by an eccentric American with a goatee beard. 'This will never catch on', he thought to himself. And so the prototype Ping Anser putter, donated by Karsten Solheim himself, found its way into another's hands. Ah, well. Not as bad as the literary agents who rejected John Grisham's first novel. There again, bad enough ...

3. *For the Love of Golf* by Peter Dobereiner

No book was better titled and no man wrote more elegantly about his chosen sport. Dobereiner was so gifted a man that several fields could have claimed him and it is golf's inestimable good fortune that he settled upon the Royal and Ancient game. He was my journalistic hero in my teenage years, his daily reports for the *Guardian* and the *Observer* being cherished reading. For example: 'If anything I have written should persuade you to try Irish golf for yourself, please do not rush at once. That would ruin everything. Pick a companion, or two or three. And take care to choose men whose drinking rate corresponds with your own. Then sneak across quietly in twos or threes and sample the game as it should be played. As it was in the beginning – world without end (if we are lucky).' If you don't enjoy this anthology of some of his finest work then seek out another game.

4. *Four Iron in the Soul* by Lawrence Donegan

Donegan is a journalist on the *Guardian* who took a year's sabbatical to caddy for the journeyman

Scottish professional Ross Drummond. The result is a funny and perceptive Hornbyesque look at both the cockeyed world of the bag carrier but also their employers.

The miracle is that Drummond even improved under Donegan's handling, to the extent of qualifying to play in the Open Championship at Lytham. 'The proudest moment of my sporting life', Donegan says. Paralysed with excitement, he walked into a pub on the day before the first round and bought a round for a couple of caddies. 'You can call yourself a real caddie now', one of them told him.

Donegan almost fainted with pride.

5. *World Atlas of Golf*
by Pat Ward-Thomas, Herbert Warren-Wind, Charles Price and Peter Thomson

It is only right that I declare an interest here. This book first came out in 1976 and has just been updated. It was I who did the updating. Please, however, don't let that put you off. I know this book is one of the great golf books precisely because I spent so much time editing it.

All the most revered courses are here, beautifully described by three of the literary giants in Ward-Thomas, Price and Warren-Wind, while Thomson adds the enthusiastic eye of a sympathetic architect. 'What makes Augusta National so great?' Warren-Wind asks rhetorically. 'It is great because it is the least obvious championship layout in America, perhaps matched nowhere in the world except by the Old course at St Andrews. Like all great courses, it must be played mentally from the green back to the tee before a single shot is hit. Since the greens are so fast, three-putting is a real hazard, no matter where the flagstick is placed. A shot to the green must be finely guaged and truly struck, or else it will bound and roll unimpeded across yards of green, making three-putting a staggering reality. Since getting close to the flagstick with approach shots is not only the easiest way of getting a par but very often the only way, the angle at which the green is approached is a constantly critical problem.

'In other words, Augusta has made many a ball-hitter look and feel a fool. For the first time he discovers that a golf course can hit him back.'

Other Recommended Books

My Life and Soft Times by Henry Longhurst
A Good Walk Spoiled by John Feinstein
PG Wodehouse: *The Golf Omnibus*
Preferred Lies by Peter Dobereiner
The Essential Henry Longhurst
Following Through: Herbert Warren-Wind on Golf

Two Essential Videos

1. *Tin Cup*

A funny, wise film about golf: who would have thought it? John Daly, Craig Stadler and Peter Jacobsen are among those with bit parts as the golf-mad Kevin Costner stars as a struggling driving range professional who finds himself contending for the United States Open. Not quite as good as Costner's two baseball films, *Bull Durham* and *Field of Dreams*, but still highly watchable.

2. *Follow the Sun*

Yes it's old and schmaltzy and it would have been much better if they had waited until after 1953 when he won three major championships. But the life story of Ben Hogan reads like a movie script and this film, made in 1951, tells the story of his struggling years, his horrific car accident and his epic struggle to overcome near-fatal injuries before returning in fairytale fashion at Riviera, one of his favourite clubs and home of the Los Angeles Open.

Recommended Titles

Highlight videos for virtually every major championship and Ryder Cup staged over the last 15 years are now available. If you are new to the sport there are a number of compilation tapes that will make fascinating viewing. Just don't let the fashions of the period put you off.

Three Essential Web Sites

1. www.golfweb.com

Its hype line is 'everything golf on the world wide web' and for once the hype is no exaggeration. Everything that is happening in golf is posted on this site. There's tournament reports, columns, access to many other web sites, news stories, an archive, details on over 20,000 courses, holiday golf: heck, it would be easier to list what isn't available.

2. www.cnnsi.com

As the internet code indicates, this site is run jointly by the CNN network and *Sports Illustrated* magazine. It covers all sports but there is a comprehensive section dedicated to golf and very good it is too. Alongside the agency reports on tournament play there are dedicated web stories on the issues of the day. This site is nowhere near as comprehensive as golfweb's – it does not seek to be – but easily outscores the former in terms of quality writing.

3. www.golfonline.com

I like this site because there are no graphics and there is no wait at all while your computer loads up the images. It is a digest of the American magazine *Golfweek*, which has improved immensely over the past two years. The news digest is excellent, as are some of the features.

Other Useful Website Addresses

Organisations

Royal and Ancient Golf Club of St Andrews: www.r&a-org.com
European Tour: www.europeantour.com
US Tour: www.pgatour.com

Players

Tiger Woods: www.tigerwoods.com
John Daly: www.gripitandripit.com
Ernie Els: www.ernie.com
Jack Nicklaus: www.nicklaus.com

Four Golf Magazines Worth Buying

Golf Monthly: The world's oldest golf magazine and among the most readable. The surveys always say that golfers want loads of instruction but editor Colin Callander has remained steadfast in his belief that people also want to know about every other aspect of the sport, and more power to him. Recently revamped, with some good new columnists on board.

Golf World: Beautifully laid out and quite often the content matches up to the glossy packaging. Have always refused to give away golf balls on the front cover like the other magazines, and it is a tribute to everyone involved that sales have never drifted away as a result.

Golf Digest: This American publication is the world's market leader in terms of sales, and probably editorial too. It has the clout that others lack and even the superstars are flattered if *Digest* comes calling, asking for an interview. Excellent columnists in Dan Jenkins and the peerless Tom Callahan.

Golf World: Same title as the British publication but this American weekly is completely different in content. All you need to know about tournament golf and tournament golfers is here, brought to you by excellent writers such as Tom Rosaforte and Bob Verdi.

Derek Lawrenson is golf correspondent of the *Sunday Telegraph*. He also writes for the *Financial Times* and has previously worked for both the *Guardian* and the *Observer.*

He is a regular contributor to *Golf Monthly* in the UK and for *Golf* magazine in the USA. His work has also appeared in numerous other golf magazines around the world. He is the author of several golf books, including the *Dream Ryder Cup*, a fantasy match featuring the best players to turn out for Europe and America.

Derek once held a one handicap and played for Lancashire at junior level. He now plays off eight and is a member of Moor Hall Golf Club, Sutton Coldfield, in the West Midlands.

He is married to Paula and they have one young son, Conor. In 1998 he had his sixth and most lucrative hole in one: it won him a Lamborghini Diablo. The car has been sold but the proceeds live on.

Inside the Game
THE ESSENTIAL GUIDE TO SPECTATOR SPORT

This new series is designed to provide a complete overview of the major world sports for the rapidly-expanding spectator market, covering the history, the rules, the main terms, how the sport is played, the great stars and teams, the sport today and the future.

Intelligently written by leading sports journalists, the books are aimed at the passionate but discerning new sports fan. They take an alternative perspective to other sports titles, going beyond the normally bland observations and reflections of the commentator and professional sportsperson, providing readers with an informed and cliché-free framework within which to understand and appreciate the great sporting dramas.

Titles currently available:

Inside the Game: **Cricket** by Rob Steen
ISBN 1 84046 031 8

Inside the Game: **Golf** by Derek Lawrenson
ISBN 1 84046 030 X

Inside the Game: **Football** by Chris Nawrat
ISBN 1 84046 028 8

Inside the Game: **Boxing** by Harry Mullan
ISBN 1 84046 029 6

Titles for 1999:

Rugby Union, Formula 1, Horse Racing

INDEX

advertising *see* sponsorship
advice rule 37
America *see* USA and golf
Augusta National 76, 83–4, 104

ball 15–18, 70
  gutta percha 13
  lost 40, 42
  out of bounds 42
  play as it lies rule 38
  unplayable 42
Ballesteros, Seve 100, 117, 120–1
Beck, Chip 109–10
books, essential 165–8
bunker
  play, Gary Player 122–3
  rules 38
business interests, golf stars 132–7

championships, major 157
cheating 27
chipping 120–1
Cink, Stewart 150–1
clothing 142–3
clubs *see under* golf
computer games 141–2
Couples, Fred 98–9, 120
Crans-sur-Sierre 88

draw 116–17
driving, experts in 118–19
dropped shot 68
Dubai Desert Classic 85
Dunhill Cup 80–1
Duval, David 147–8

Els, Ernie 97–8, 109, 145–7
Emirates Course 84–5
equipment 138–40
errors 32–6
etiquette 43–7

fade 116–17
Faldo, Nick 99, 107–8, 128–9
Finchem, Tim 124, 126
fourball 156
foursomes 156

fourteen-club limit 14
Furyk, Jim 97–8, 111–12

Garcia, Sergio 151
Garrido, Ignacio 149–50
glossary of terms 51–65
golf
  bag 18, 68–9
  balls *see* ball
  clubs 13–14, 19, 69, 138–9, 140
  courses 12, 20–1
  growth in 124–6
  origins 7–11
  simulated 141–2
  and television 126–9
golfing terms *see* glossary of terms
greensomes 156
gutta percha ball 13

Haskell ball 13, 15–16
Home Golf Unions 75
Honourable Company of Edinburgh
  Golfers 9

income, golfing stars 132–5
internet 141
irons 13
    see also long irons; short irons

Jacklin, Tony 160
Janzen, Lee 111–12

Leonard, Justin 100, 148–9
LGU 75
Loch Lomond 89–90
long irons 119
lost ball 40, 42
LPGA Tour 73

Masters, The 76, 107–8, 109–10
matchplay 114
McCormack 132–3
Mickelson, Phil 149
mind, power of 94
Mize, Larry 158
Montgomerie, Colin 118

Nicklaus, Jack 25–6, 107, 132–3, 157–8, 159
Norman, Greg 132, 134–5, 137, 162

Olazabal, Jose-Maria 98–9, 120
Open Championship 11, 76, 107, 110–11
order of play rule 37–8
organisations 71–80
origins of golf 7–11
Ouimet, Francis 22–3
out-of-bounds ball 42

Palmer, Arnold 24–5, 132–3, 136, 159
Parnevik, Jesper 110–11
Pebble Beach 81–2
PGA 72
    of America 73
    Championship 77
    Tour 72–3
    youth drive 128
PGAET 71–2
pitching 120–1
play as it lies rule 38
Player, Gary 122–3
practice rule 36
President's Cup 115
prize money 11
putting 39–40, 123

Reid, John 10
Royal and Ancient 9
rules 27–32, 36–43
Ryder Cup 11, 77–8, 120–1, 163

Sarazen, Gene 23–4
short irons 119–20
simulated golf 141–2
skins 156
slow play 47
Spain see Valderrama
sponsorship 129–31, 142–3
St Andrews 8, 10, 74, 80–1, 107
    see also Royal and Ancient
Stableford 156
steel shaft 14

strategy 102–6
strokeplay 113–14
    tournament 153
swing 92–3, 97–100
Switzerland see Crans-sur-Sierre

Taylor Made clubs 139
team golf 115
tee 15
television and golf 126–9
terms 51–65
tours 152
    see also LPGA Tour; PGA Tour; World Tour
Trevino, Lee 162
Turnberry 87, 110–11

United States, game arrives 10
unplayable ball 42
US Open 11, 76–7, 82, 109
USA and golf 127, 129
USGA 9, 10, 75

Valderrama 85–6, 111–12, 153
videos 168–9
Volvo Championship 79–80

water hazard 40–1
Watson, Tom 161
weather, poor 112–13
web sites 141, 169–70
West Course 86–7
Westwood, Lee 148
women 101
    see also LGU; WPGET
wood 6
    see also golf clubs
Woods, Tiger 118–19, 124–6, 145–7
Work, Bertram 15
World
    Championship 85, 153
    Cup 153
    Series 153
    Tour 152
WPGET 73–4

youth and golf 143